SHERRIE HEWSON

Nana's Kitchen

SHERRIE HEWSON

Nana's Kitchen

Over 100 Delicious Family Recipes

MACMILLAN

First published 2014 by Macmillan
an imprint of Pan Macmillan, a division of Macmillan Publishers Limited
Pan Macmillan, 20 New Wharf Road, London N1 9RR
Basingstoke and Oxford
Associated companies throughout the world
www.panmacmillan.com

ISBN 978-1-4472-4773-9

A CIP catalogue record for this book is available from
the British Library.

Art Direction, Styling and Page Design: Simon Daley at Giraffe Books
Copy Editing: Salima Hirani at Giraffe Books
Cover and Author Photography: Nicky Johnston
Food Photography: Tony Briscoe
Food Styling: Clare Greenstreet

Printed in Italy by Rotolito Lombarda SpA

Contents

This book is for all the nanas and very nearly nanas and future nanas, whatever you are called. I've heard Nana, Nunu, Namby, Gran, Granny, Grandma, Gramma and even Gouchy or Gummy! I always called my maternal grandmother Nana, and that's what my grandchildren now call me. But as my nana used to say, 'It doesn't matter what they call me as long as they don't call me late for my dinner!'

So, all you nanas out there, your country needs you. Dinner – from preparing it to eating it, all round the table together – is a vital part of being a good grandmother. My nana was a constant source of peace, unconditional love, security and good food. I needed her, her wisdom and her hugs. Her home smelt warm, she smelt wonderful and her kitchen smelt magical.

Some of my happiest days were spent in Nana's kitchen and, sometimes, my Great Grandma Birtles – Nana's mother – would be there, too. They would bicker over who did what and there was never really enough space for the two of them but, even as a tiny child, I used to mediate between them – probably because I was always the apple of their eyes – without even knowing that that was what I was doing.

Now that I'm a nana myself, to Olly, who is seven, and Molly, who's just turned three – and, yes, they are the apples of my eye – I want to give them a taste of the things I enjoyed as a child and to show them that cooking good food is both easy and fun. Life today is so fast, with everyone having to work all hours. Life was so much simpler back then. It sounds like a cliché, but it's true; life was slower, there was time to sit in the garden and shell peas. I showed Olly and Molly how to do this just the other day and they were thrilled to see baby peas asleep in their pods. Time is the best thing we can give our grandchildren; nanas have much more time than busy mums and dads. Plenty of time is what my nana gave to me and I've never forgotten the things we shared.

I bought my grandchildren a butterfly house the other day. It was just a box filled with caterpillars, that's all. But you watched the house for five days, then turned the caterpillars into a small netted cage where they clung as chrysalises for another five days, then we watched as they turned into butterflies, and then, after that, we released them and watched them fly into the garden. Olly and Molly were mesmerised and, I must say, it was magical. Kids are bombarded with technology, so it's up to us – the nana army – to reveal to them the pleasure to be had in simple things. I know it's easier said than done, but it is doable, believe me. I have a great photo of Molly covered in flour, sitting on

the worktop stirring a cake mixture, happy as the day is long. And when Olly sees a cake rising in the oven, he just loves it.

Food is a leveller. It has no class barrier, language barrier or taboo. It used to be important in schools; now, sadly, domestic science, as it was called in my day, seems largely to have disappeared from the school curriculum. All the health-and-safety nonsense and EU rulings, I guess. When I was five, I had a gang of friends and we would run down by the river all day long in muck and rain, snow and slush, be frozen and filthy, but so happy. It wasn't dangerous and it helped to mould us into well-rounded people. And we came out of school knowing how to cook scrambled eggs and one or two other things.

When I was a child, we might not have had the eclectic range of things in the shops that we have now, but the food was good, without processing, colouring, antibiotics. That said, today's choice is amazing and I love using ingredients such as chilli, coriander, mangoes and limes. You never saw these in the greengrocers when I was growing up. But you can keep your wheatgrass shots. I had one once and it was the most disgusting thing I have ever tasted and made me feel quite ill. I was fine before! Yet give me a bowl of bananas in custard and I feel on top of the world. And my dad was only truly happy when he had a Yorkshire pudding with mash and beef gravy in front of him. His face would be void of stress and a look of pure contentment would linger for quite some time.

So remember your secret pleasures, your on-your-own treats. We've all got them. And as long as you don't live exclusively on bananas and custard (though it might be tempting), or thickly buttered buns, a little of what you fancy really will do you good. The same goes for our kids. They should learn to cook so that they can make the things they love to eat and to understand how wonderful ingredients can be turned into a fabulous meal. Cooking should be creative, theatrical and – above all – great fun. Cooking's not rocket science. You can cook ambitious cheffy things if you want to – I did just that on the TV show *Masterchef* and was really rather good at it, too – but here I wanted to give you recipes that the whole family can enjoy, the kind of comforting family meals I grew up with, cooked with love by my nana and my mother, which you can now share with your family, especially the grandchildren. Why buy scones when you can make them in just a few minutes and enjoy them fresh from the oven?

So, nanas of the world, let's start a movement to recruit our grandchildren – no matter how young they are – to cook with us. Let's give them dollops of time, lashings of love and oodles of food for a happy life. Join us in making a mess, making food and making fun.

Brilliant Breakfasts

I get so excited about breakfast. The luscious smell of cinnamon, a munchy muffin, the silkiness of scrambled eggs – just me, Olly and Molly in our jim-jams, all cosy and cuddled up having brekkie … A far cry from a 5 a.m. call for filming *Benidorm*, feeling cold and sleepy in the make-up chair, squinting into the mirror, with the make-up artist despairing as she picks up a big, fluffy brush, sipping weak tea and eating soggy toast, hiding so that the gorgeous Jake Canuso (who plays Mateo) doesn't see you until you are fully made up and ready to dazzle.

But you don't need your make-up on to make these yummy first bites of the day. And breakfast needn't be the same every day – mix it up and try something new!

Simple Scrambled Eggs

This was one of the first things I learnt to cook. The secret is to love your eggs and use a lot of butter! And scrambled eggs can be jazzed up with the greatest of ease. Try adding any of the following to the eggs just before they're ready to serve: torn basil and grated Parmesan; chopped chorizo; chopped smoked salmon; chopped spring onions and coriander; cubes of bacon, fried with a few thinly sliced mushrooms; little cubes of fried potato; or a pinch of curry powder. The possibilities are endless!

Serves 4

8 eggs
60g butter
120ml milk
Sea salt and freshly ground black pepper

Crack the eggs into a bowl and whisk. You need to get as much air in as possible to ensure your scramble is light and fluffy, so get stuck in.

Melt 25g of the butter in the pan you'll use to cook the eggs. Pour the melted butter into the beaten egg with the milk, and season with salt and pepper. Whisk again – and enjoy!

Put the remaining butter into the pan and set it over a lowish heat. When the butter has melted and is hot enough (common sense will tell you when it's ready), pour the egg mixture into the pan. Now here comes the love and understanding. Don't mess with the eggs too much – let them enjoy the butter. Then, after they have settled, start to gently fold the eggs with a plastic spatula. Keep turning and slowly folding until the liquid egg has begun to firm up. But don't wait too long – they will tell you themselves when they are done.

Turn off the heat, still lifting the eggs gently around the pan, adjust the seasoning, then let them be. The residual heat in the pan will finish off the cooking for you. Finally, pour the scrambled eggs gently onto a plate and serve. Gorgeous!

Bursting Blueberry Muffins

Blueberries are so good for you! And they're delicious in these muffins, which are perfect for a quick breakfast or with a mid-morning cup of coffee. But if you're not mad about them, you can ring the changes very easily; simply use raspberries, apricots or walnuts instead. Or make muffins that are more of a teatime treat by adding chopped chocolate or chocolate chips, marshmallows, chopped cinder toffee or honeycomb, even chunks of Turkish delight or a dollop or two of your favourite jam. You can make savoury muffins, too. Drop the sugar from the list of ingredients and stir in 100g grated cheese instead.

Makes 12

225g plain flour
75g caster sugar
2 teaspoons baking powder
150ml milk
50ml sunflower oil
1 egg, lightly beaten
Handful of blueberries
2 bananas, chopped
50g soft light brown sugar

Preheat the oven to 190°C/fan 170°C/gas mark 5. Line a 12-hole muffin tin with paper muffin cases.

Mix the flour, sugar and baking powder in a bowl. Add the milk, sunflower oil, egg and fruit. Stir quickly until the ingredients are all incorporated, but don't overmix.

Spoon the mixture into the muffin cases and sprinkle with the light brown sugar. Bake for 15–20 minutes until the muffins have risen and they are springy to the touch.

Glorious Granola

Now this is a much better way to start the day than with all those sugary cereals you buy in the supermarket. My glorious granola will keep for about a month in a sealed container – if it lasts that long. Serve it with cold milk or yogurt. It makes a great topping for ice cream, too, although perhaps not for breakfast!

Makes 12–15 servings (depending on how hungry or greedy you are!)

2 tablespoons vegetable oil

125ml maple syrup

2 tablespoons honey

300g rolled oats

50g sunflower seeds

4 tablespoons sesame seeds

50g pumpkin seeds

50g hazelnuts

50g almonds

50g coconut flakes

50g raisins

50g dried cranberries

Preheat the oven to 150°C/fan 130°C/gas mark 2.

Mix the oil, maple syrup and honey in a bowl. Add the oats, seeds and nuts and mix well.

Spread out the granola across 2 greased baking sheets. Bake for 15 minutes. Add the coconut and dried fruit, stir them into the mixture well, and bake for another 10–15 minutes until the oats are golden and the nuts are nicely toasted. Leave to cool for 5 minutes, then break up any large clumps. Now leave the granola to cool completely. Store it in an airtight container.

Savoury Cheese Bread

This tasty cheese bread is delicious on its own or with a bowl of soup. The recipe is very versatile and can be easily adapted to suit your own tastes. I love mixing sweet and savoury, so a cheese loaf with cinnamon butter is my idea of heaven. Or you could drop the cheese and use pieces of dried fruit – peaches, apricots, mango, pineapple, raisins – or nuts and seeds, or a combination of them all. Whatever flavour you go for, the bread makes a fabulous breakfast warm from the oven, cut into thick slices and generously buttered.

Makes 2 loaves

500g strong white bread flour, plus extra for dusting

1 x 7g sachet of easy blend dried yeast

1½ teaspoons salt

25g butter

115g mature Cheddar cheese, grated, plus extra grated cheese for sprinkling

300–360ml tepid water

Sunflower oil, for greasing

1 egg, beaten, for brushing

Put the flour, yeast and salt into a large bowl. Rub the butter into the flour, then stir in the cheese. Make a well in the middle and, using a round-bladed knife, stir in 300ml of the tepid water, then mix in up to 60ml more, as needed, to form a soft, slightly sticky dough.

Gather the dough into a ball and turn it out on a lightly floured surface. Knead for 8–10 minutes until it feels smooth and elastic. Shape the dough into a round. Wipe out and grease the bowl in which you mixed the dough, then put the dough ball back into it. Cover the bowl with cling film and leave it in a warm place for 1¼–2 hours until the dough has doubled in size.

Line a baking sheet with non-stick baking paper.

Turn out the dough on a lightly floured surface and knead it briefly – 3 or 4 squeezes is enough. You don't want to handle it too much at this stage. Cut the dough in half and shape each piece into a ball. Place these, well spaced apart, on the prepared baking sheet. Slash the tops several times with a sharp knife. Cover with oiled cling film and leave to rise in a warm place for 40 minutes to 1 hour.

Preheat the oven to 220°C/fan 200°C/gas mark 7.

Brush each piece of dough with beaten egg. Scatter more grated cheese over the tops. »

» Bake for 10 minutes, then reduce the heat to 200°C/fan 180°C/gas mark 6 and bake for a further 20–25 minutes until golden brown. When you think they are ready, tap the bases of the loaves. If they sound hollow, take them out of the oven and place on a wire rack to cool.

Tip-Top Cinnamon Toast

Cinnamon sugar is such a comforting food; it's like a log fire or the smell of fish and chips. It can be used on anything – rice pudding, fruit salad, or scattered over a cappuccino for instance. You could even put it in a sugar sandwich (white bread, lots of butter, white sugar) – this was a favourite when I was young but today I suspect people would find the idea quite shocking. I like it best on toast, combined with butter for a breakfast that's like a big hug. This cinnamon toast makes a lovely treat and is very simple to throw together at the last minute.

Makes 6 slices of toast

60g granulated sugar
60g butter, softened
3–4 teaspoons ground cinnamon
6 slices of white bread

Mix the sugar, butter and cinnamon together in a bowl.

Meanwhile, toast the slices of bread. When the bread is toasted, spread the butter and cinnamon sugar mixture on the hot toast. If you like, you can then flash the buttered toast under a hot grill until the sugary butter has started to melt and bubble. But don't look away while the bread is under the grill – it only takes a minute or 2 at most.

Nana O'Shaughnessy's Soda Bread

My ex-husband was born in Ireland, which is why my daughter Keeley has an Irish name. It means 'the beautiful one' and she most certainly is. And so is this gorgeous bread, which comes from the Irish side of the family.

Makes 1 loaf

Vegetable oil, for greasing
300g wholemeal flour, plus extra for dusting
5 tablespoons caster sugar
1½ teaspoons baking powder
1 teaspoon salt
¾ teaspoon bicarbonate of soda
50g butter, chilled and cubed
240ml buttermilk
130g raisins
70g sunflower seeds (or use whichever seeds you prefer)
Butter, honey or jam, to serve

Preheat the oven to 190°C/fan 170°C/gas mark 5. Grease a 20cm cake or loaf tin with a little vegetable oil.

Sift the flour in a large bowl, then add 4 tablespoons of the sugar, the baking powder, salt and bicarbonate of soda. Add the butter and, using your fingertips, rub it into the flour until the mixture resembles coarse breadcrumbs.

Make a well in the centre of the mixture and pour in the buttermilk. Gradually stir the dry mixture into the buttermilk until all the ingredients are well blended, then mix in the raisins and sunflower seeds.

Using floured hands, shape the dough into a ball. Transfer the dough to the prepared tin, flatten the top slightly, then sprinkle over the remaining sugar.

Bake for about 40 minutes until the crust is brown. To check if the bread is cooked through, insert a skewer into the centre – it should come out clean. If not, give the bread another 5–10 minutes in the oven.

Leave the bread to cool in the tin for 10 minutes, then transfer to a wire rack.

Serve warm, with butter, honey or jam.

Dutch Apple Pancake

We all love pancakes and they are not just for Pancake Day, although I do love having a special day for them. There isn't anything that doesn't go in or on a pancake – savoury, sweet or plain – and homemade pancakes are so moreish. This dish is great to have with the kids but can also make a rather romantic breakfast for two – especially if you wash it down with a Bellini. A couple of glasses of that lovely champagne and peach cocktail and love would really be in the air!

Serves 4

150g plain flour
1 teaspoon baking powder
2 eggs
150ml buttermilk
3 tablespoons cold water
1 tablespoon butter or sunflower oil
1 dessert apple, peeled and sliced
Mint leaves, to garnish (optional)
Greek yogurt, to serve (optional)

Stir the flour and the baking powder together in a bowl.

In a separate bowl, whisk the eggs with the buttermilk and cold water. Pour the wet ingredients into the dry mixture and beat well to make a smooth batter.

Heat the butter or oil in a frying pan and add the apple slices. Cook over a medium-low heat for several minutes until the apple begins to soften and brown slightly. Pour the pancake mix over the apple and cook for about 3 minutes until the underside is golden brown, then flip over the pancake to cook the other side for the same amount of time.

Turn out the pancake on a plate and garnish with mint leaves. Serve it in thick slices as it comes, or with a dollop of Greek yogurt.

Lovely Lunches

We all fancy a treat in the middle of the day and I'm a firm believer in the old phrase 'a little of what you fancy does you good'. Cooking up a storm for lunch can feed both body and soul.

About a hundred years ago, when cooking was the last thing on my mind, I had rather an exciting lunch proposal! I was making a film with the gorgeous Harrison Ford. All the girls were besotted with him and one day, when we were sitting waiting to film, he turned to me and very quietly said, 'Hey, would you like to have lunch with me tomorrow?' I managed to mumble, 'Oh, yes please,' but I was so gobsmacked, I didn't know where to put myself. I bought an outfit that I couldn't afford and the girls on the set did my hair and make-up. He'd said 1 p.m. at the Italian restaurant near the studio. I arrived, terrified. The maître d' welcomed me, saying, 'Miss Hewson? Follow me …' He showed me to a back room and opened the door – and there was Harrison, with twelve other ladies sitting at the table! They all laughed and clapped and my only consolation was that I got to sit next to him!

The recipes in this chapter will give you lots of enjoyment, whether you're treating yourself, or are serving up an intimate Harrison Ford-style lunch for twelve!

Sweet Tomato and
Roasted Pepper Soup

Soup and good bread to dunk in it make a fabulous lunch. Soups really don't take long to make – this one can be on the table in half an hour. I've found that kids love this dish, too, so it's a winner all round.

Serves 4

1 red pepper, deseeded and chopped into largish pieces
1 yellow pepper, deseeded and chopped into largish pieces
1 small red onion, peeled and quartered
2 garlic cloves, peeled
12 cherry tomatoes, stalks removed
1 tablespoon olive oil
500ml vegetable stock (or use stock cubes)
Sea salt and freshly ground black pepper
Pinch of cayenne pepper (optional)

To serve
Single cream
Chopped chives

Preheat the oven to 180°C/fan 160°C/gas mark 4.

Place the peppers, onion, garlic and tomatoes in a large baking tray, drizzle with the oil and roast for 15 minutes.

Remove the vegetables from the oven and tip them into a large saucepan. Add the stock and seasoning (add the cayenne now, too, if you're using it), bring to the boil, then simmer for 10 minutes.

Take the pan off the heat and blend the mixture in a food processor or with a hand-blender until smooth.

Serve in soup bowls with a swirl of cream and a sprinkling of chopped chives.

Peasouper Soup

Some old recipe books call this deliciously filling soup London Particular, because it's as thick as the 'peasouper' fogs that enveloped London in Victorian times. When I was a child it was always made with the stock that came from boiling a bit of gammon or bacon, and with split peas that you had to soak overnight. My version uses leftover ham (or buy good thick slices) and frozen peas. It's *much* quicker and easier to prepare and is every bit as good.

Serves 4

1 tablespoon vegetable oil
1 onion, peeled and finely chopped
150g frozen peas
1 bay leaf
1 litre ham stock (homemade or use stock cubes)
200g cooked ham, torn into strips

Heat the oil in a saucepan. Add the onion and cook over a low heat until it's soft and translucent. Add the peas, bay leaf and the stock, bring to the boil, then simmer for 10–15 minutes.

Remove the pan from the heat, discard the bay leaf and blend the soup to a thick purée in a food processor or with a hand-blender.

Return the soup to the pan and add half the ham. Bring the mixture back to the boil, then pour the soup into serving bowls. Garnish with the remaining ham and serve immediately.

Brilliant Bacon and Sweetcorn Chowder

Chowders are much easier to make than they sound. They are basically stews made with cream or milk, and are so fulfilling and warming – a proper tummycuddler. I'm not sure that's even a word but you know what I mean!

Serves 4

50g butter
100g bacon, diced
1 onion, peeled and diced
2 celery sticks, chopped
1 leek, trimmed and thinly sliced
1 tablespoon plain flour
240ml chicken stock
1 large potato, peeled and diced
210g can sweetcorn, drained
240ml milk
Sea salt and freshly ground black pepper
Pinch of cayenne pepper
2 tablespoons single or double cream

Melt 25g of the butter in a large saucepan and cook the bacon in it for 2–3 minutes or until it browns. Add the onion, celery and leek and cook, stirring constantly, for a further 2 minutes. Now add the flour and stir well to combine it with the vegetables. Pour in the stock, add the potato and bring to the boil, then simmer for 20 minutes.

Add the sweetcorn and milk and simmer for a further 3 minutes. Season with salt, pepper and cayenne. Stir in the cream and heat the mixture through, but do not allow it to boil. Stir in the remaining butter just before serving.

Nutty Southern Squash Soup

This soup, made with sweet potato, pumpkin and peanut butter, is deliciously spicy – and you can add more chilli if you think you can take the heat! You need some really good bread to serve it with. And butter – lashings of it, as the Famous Five might have said, even though having lots of butter is frowned upon these days. But a little bit of what you fancy …

Serves 6

30g butter
1 onion, peeled and chopped
2 garlic cloves, peeled and crushed
½ teaspoon mild curry powder
½ teaspoon ground coriander
¼ teaspoon chopped red chilli
250–300g pumpkin or butternut squash, peeled and cubed
250g sweet potato, peeled and cubed
1 litre vegetable stock
½ teaspoon salt
2 tablespoons peanut butter

To serve
Single cream or natural yogurt
Handful of coriander leaves, chopped

Heat the butter in a saucepan. Add the onion and garlic and cook over a low heat until the onion is soft and translucent.

Add the ground spices and chopped chilli to the pan. Cook, stirring, for a few seconds, then add the pumpkin and sweet potato. Mix them thoroughly with the spicy onion mixture. Pour in the stock, bring to the boil, then simmer for 15 minutes until the vegetables are tender.

Add the salt and peanut butter to the pan. Take the pan off the heat and blend the mixture in a food processor or with a hand-blender until smooth. (If you prefer, just mash the vegetables into the stock to give the soup a chunkier texture.) Adjust the seasoning to taste.

Ladle the soup into serving bowls, drizzle over the cream or dollop in the yogurt, sprinkle with chopped coriander and serve immediately.

Homely Leek and Potato Soup

Warming and homely, this dish is an absolute classic – and so easy to make. It's not surprising that the French name for it means 'Good Wife Soup'! Try it for lunch on a crisp winter's day after a brisk walk – it'll fill you up nicely and you'll be full steam ahead all afternoon.

Serves 4

1 large baking potato, peeled
25g butter
2 leeks, trimmed and sliced
1 litre chicken stock (homemade or use stock cubes)
1 bay leaf
Sea salt and freshly ground black pepper

To serve
Single cream
Handful of chives, chopped

Cut the peeled potato in half lengthways, then slice the halves into pieces the thickness of a pound coin.

Heat the butter in a saucepan and, when it just begins to sizzle, add the vegetables. Turn them in the butter to coat them then cook gently for about 5 minutes.

Pour the stock into the pan, add the bay leaf, season with salt and pepper and bring to the boil, then simmer gently for about 20 minutes or until the potatoes are completely cooked.

Take the pan off the heat, discard the bay leaf and blend the mixture in a food processor or with a hand-blender until smooth. Serve immediately with a swirl of cream and a sprinkling of chopped chives.

Smoked Salmon Platter with Pickles

A salmon has a long way to travel in life and struggles to the end, leaping over every obstacle. So give its life respect and serve it beautifully, with love, so at least it could have said, 'Well, that was worth it.' This dish is a beautiful way of presenting salmon. If you can, buy wild salmon, but if you can only get hold of the farmed variety, ensure it's organic. Salad goes well with the salmon, and I like to dress the leaves with a zingy vinaigrette with a good balance of sweet and tart. But I think salad dressings are a personal thing, so use your favourite if you prefer.

Serves 4

320g thinly sliced smoked salmon
Handful of gherkins, finely chopped
Handful of capers, finely chopped
½ red onion, peeled and
   finely chopped
2 red chillies, deseeded and chopped
Coarse-grain mustard, to taste
1 bag of mixed salad leaves

For the raspberry vinaigrette
Pinch of salt
½ teaspoon Dijon mustard
½ teaspoon honey
1 teaspoon brown sugar (optional)
1 tablespoon balsamic vinegar
2 tablespoons olive oil
1 garlic clove, peeled and crushed
Handful of raspberries, crushed

First make the vinaigrette. Put all the ingredients into a jar, screw on the lid and shake well to blend them thoroughly. Adjust the seasoning and sweetness to taste. Set aside.

Carefully place the salmon in small coils on 4 beautiful individual platters. Divide the gherkins, capers, onion and chillies into 4 equal portions. Using 1 portion per platter, surround the coils of salmon on each platter with the mixture, in little heaps. Add a small blob of mustard to each serving.

Put the salad leaves in a bowl and use 1 tablespoon of the vinaigrette to dress them. Now add a small salad of the pretty leaves to each helping and serve immediately.

Wild Salmon Carpaccio with Guacamole

Raw fish is so not me, but when I was filming *Benidorm* in Spain it was a popular local dish, so of course I had to try it – and I sort of liked it in the end! There, it was served up with dill mayonnaise, but life's a bit too short to make mayonnaise so just use a good ready-made brand and add chopped dill leaves. However, I much prefer my homemade guacamole to shop-bought products. Again, always try to buy wild salmon rather than farmed but, in any case, ensure it's spankingly fresh.

Serves 6–8

800g salmon fillet

For the dressing
2 garlic cloves, peeled and crushed
1 teaspoon soft light brown sugar
Juice of 1 lemon
1 teaspoon salt
½ teaspoon freshly ground black pepper
1½ tablespoons olive oil (I use a lemon-infused oil that makes this dish extra delicious, but ordinary olive oil is fine)

For the guacamole
2 avocados, peeled, stoned and roughly chopped

2 garlic cloves, peeled and crushed
Grated zest and juice of 2 limes
1 tablespoon sesame seeds (if you want to, toast them in the oven for a few minutes)
1 red chilli, deseeded and finely chopped
1 spring onion, chopped (use some of the green bit for colour)
Olive oil, to taste
Handful of basil leaves, torn, plus extra to serve
Sea salt and freshly ground black pepper
½ tablespoon capers, plus extra to serve

Rinse and dry the salmon, then wrap it tightly in cling film and leave it in the fridge for 1 hour, which will make it much easier to slice.

Mix all the dressing ingredients together.

Take the salmon out of the fridge, unwrap it and place it on a chopping board. Using a very, very sharp knife, cut it into the thinnest possible slices. Lay the slices beautifully across a serving platter and drizzle with the dressing.

Cover the platter with cling film and return it to the fridge for about ½ hour. (Obviously, all this can be done well in advance.)

To make the guacamole, put all the ingredients into a bowl and mix well, but don't overdo it – I like it rough and chunky. Garnish it with a little extra torn basil and a few more capers.

Serve the salmon platter with the guacamole on the side.

Sunny Salade Niçoise

The proper ingredients for a Niçoise salad are always up for debate. People add all sorts to it, but I think it should taste clean and fresh. It should be neat and crunchy and preferably eaten under a hot blue sky with a cold glass of wine.

Serves 4

1 Cos lettuce, washed and torn into bite-size pieces
8 new potatoes, cooked and thickly sliced
125g French beans, trimmed and cooked
4 tomatoes, quartered
130g can tuna, drained
6 anchovy fillets

4 eggs, boiled for 6 minutes, halved
Handful of pitted black olives

For the dressing
½ teaspoon Dijon mustard
1 tablespoon red wine vinegar
3 tablespoons olive oil
1 garlic clove, peeled and crushed
Sea salt and freshly ground black pepper

To make the dressing, put all the ingredients into a jar, screw on the lid and shake vigorously.

Get your prettiest salad bowl out and fill it with the lettuce. Scatter the potatoes, beans, tomatoes, tuna and anchovy fillets over the lettuce. Drizzle over the dressing. Surround the salad with the boiled egg halves and scatter black olives over the top. Serve immediately.

Mellow Mackerel Pâté

Well, I say mellow, but the chilli really gives this a delicious kick. But then I like things a bit spicy. If you don't, just leave it out. This pâté makes a great little lunch served with crisp toast and a green salad.

Serves 4

3 smoked mackerel fillets
100g crème fraîche
150g cream cheese
1 red chilli, deseeded and chopped
1 garlic clove, peeled and crushed
2 spring onions, green and white parts finely chopped
Sea salt and freshly ground black pepper
Squeeze of lemon or lime juice
Pinch of turmeric (optional)
Chopped chives
Toast, bread, oatcakes or crackers, to serve

Skin the mackerel fillets, check them for bones, then flake the fish into a bowl.

Add the crème fraîche, cheese, chilli, garlic and spring onions and mix thoroughly. Mix in the seasoning, a squeeze of lemon or lime juice, the turmeric (if using) and chopped chives to taste. You don't want to make the mixture too smooth; it should be chunky.

Cover the bowl with cling film and chill in the fridge until you're ready to serve the pâté.

Serve with toast, fresh bread (an onion loaf would be lovely with this pâté), oatcakes or sesame crackers.

Posh Prosciutto and Melon

I'm all for melons – do you know how good they are for you? Check it out: they're good for digestion, the kidneys, the heart and blood pressure, they help to alleviate the common cold and they give you a face lift at the same time … OK, I made that last bit up, sorry. But it was a nice try.

Serves 4

1 small, ripe cantaloupe melon
1 bag of baby salad leaves
6 slices of prosciutto, cut into strips

Sea salt and freshly ground
   black pepper
120ml olive oil

For the dressing
2 teaspoons honey
1 teaspoon Dijon mustard
60ml freshly squeezed lime juice

To garnish
1 kiwi fruit, chopped
6 strawberries, sliced

Halve the melon, remove the seeds and scoop out the flesh with a melon baller.

Arrange the salad leaves on a platter and put the melon balls on top. Scatter the strips of prosciutto over the melon.

Mix the dressing ingredients together and drizzle the dressing over the salad. Garnish with some chopped kiwi and strawberry slices. Chill for at least ½ hour before serving.

Sizzling Goat's Cheese and Strawberry Salad

This is a super salad, especially if you're creative with the leaves you use – there are so many varieties available nowadays. I generally go for a combination of lamb's lettuce, watercress, baby spinach, mizuna and rocket. Be adventurous! Try them all.

Serves 2

100g goat's cheese, cut into
   2 equal discs
1 tablespoon olive oil
1 garlic clove, peeled and crushed
1 red chilli, deseeded and
   finely chopped
Sea salt and freshly ground
   black pepper
1 bag of mixed salad leaves
350g strawberries

Handful of black grapes (optional)

For the strawberry vinaigrette
90g strawberries
1 tablespoon honey
2 garlic cloves, peeled and crushed
2 tablespoons balsamic vinegar
1 teaspoon mustard
Soft light brown sugar, to taste
120ml olive oil

First make the strawberry vinaigrette. Purée the strawberries in a blender. Add the honey, garlic, vinegar and mustard and some salt, pepper and brown sugar to taste (the amount of sugar you should use depends on the sweetness of your strawberries). Mix well then add the olive oil. Blend until creamy, then taste and adjust the seasoning as necessary.

Put the goat's cheese in a bowl, drizzle with the olive oil, sprinkle over the garlic and red chilli and season with salt and pepper.

Heat a griddle pan until hot and cook the goat's cheese on it until it just begins to melt but still retains its shape. (You could also cook it under a hot grill.) Remove from the heat and keep warm.

While the cheese is cooking, make the salad. Put all the leaves in a large bowl and pour over the strawberry vinaigrette and the whole strawberries (halve them if they're very large). Mix very gently. Arrange the dressed leaves on 2 plates then lay a piece of the goat's cheese on each pile of leaves. If you want to, add a few black grapes as well. Serve immediately.

Hot Halloumi Salad

I used to go to Cyprus a lot in the 1970s. I was very young and fell in love with the Mayor of Larnaca, who was ten years older than me and very rich. My mother thought it was the perfect match, but sadly I was also in love with David Cassidy, David Essex and Paul McCartney. Mind you, the Mayor had a Weimaraner called Smokey and I really did fall in love with him. Ever since, I've had a passion for these beautiful dogs. It wasn't long before I had one of my own, called Caius.

Halloumi is something that immediately takes me back to long summer days in Cyprus. It's so versatile, keeps for a year unopened and is very healthy. And who knows, you might meet the next Mayor of Larnaca if you make this salad!

Serves 4

250g halloumi
2 avocados, peeled and cubed
1 large mango, peeled and cubed
125g cooked beetroot, cubed
½ red onion, peeled and diced
25ml olive oil
Juice of 1 lime
1 teaspoon red chilli flakes
Handful of coriander
  leaves, chopped
Sea salt and freshly
  ground black pepper

Handful of chopped toasted
  nuts (almonds or cashews
  would be nice)

For the marinade
6 tablespoons olive oil
4 garlic cloves, peeled and
  chopped
6 tablespoons lemon juice
25g mint leaves

Blitz the marinade ingredients in a blender or food processor and set aside.

Slice the halloumi to around the same thickness as shop-bought bread and put the slices into a bowl. Pour over the marinade and turn the slices over to ensure they are well covered. Cover the bowl in cling film and leave it in the fridge for at least ½ hour to allow the halloumi to marinate.

While the halloumi is marinating, make the salad. Mix the avocado, mango, beetroot and red onion in a bowl and dress with the oil, lime juice and red chilli. Add the chopped coriander and season to taste. Scatter over the nuts. Set aside.

Preheat a griddle on the hob. When it's nice and hot, remove the halloumi »

» slices from the marinade and cook them on the hot griddle for about 1 minute on each side. (Alternatively, use a non-stick frying pan.) Ideally the halloumi pieces should each have a patchy brown exterior and still be reasonably firm. Serve alongside the salad.

Easy Courgette and Bacon Quiche

You might say that this is an unusual take on a quiche – there's no pastry for a start. But do try it. It's really good and so easy to prepare.

Serves 4

120ml sunflower oil, plus extra for greasing
5 eggs, beaten
3 courgettes, grated
3 rashers of bacon, chopped
150g self-raising flour
1 large onion, peeled and thinly sliced
100g Cheddar cheese, grated (or use another strong cheese)
Sea salt and freshly ground black pepper

Preheat the oven to 180°C/fan 160°C/gas mark 4. Lightly oil a 23cm pie dish.
   Beat the oil into the beaten eggs, then add the remaining ingredients. Mix well. Pour the mixture into the prepared pie dish and bake for 30–40 minutes or until golden and cooked through. Serve immediately.

Magical Mushroom Quiche

Magical indeed! This is one of my very favourite quiches. And these days there's no need to stick to button mushrooms – there are so many varieties to choose from, you can really go to town. I like to use chanterelles, when I can find them, and oyster and chestnut mushrooms – but you decide!

Serves 4–6

1 x 23cm pre-baked pastry shell or 1 sheet ready-rolled or
   250g homemade shortcrust pastry
40g butter
2 shallots, peeled and chopped
300g mixed mushrooms, sliced
2 sprigs of thyme
6 eggs
360ml single cream
Sea salt and freshly ground black pepper
100g Parmesan cheese, grated

Preheat the oven to 190°C/fan 170°C/gas mark 5. If you're using ready-rolled or homemade pastry, line a 23cm tart tin with it, trim off the excess pastry, fill the lined tin with a layer of ceramic baking beans (or just use lentils) and bake blind for 20 minutes.

Melt the butter in a frying pan and, when it foams, add the shallots and fry gently until they are soft but not brown. Add the mushrooms and thyme and cook until the mushrooms are golden. Leave to cool slightly.

Whisk the eggs and cream together and season the mixture.

Sprinkle the bottom of the shop-bought or blind-baked pastry shell with the grated cheese, add the cooled mushrooms and pour the cream and egg mixture over the top. Bake for 25–30 minutes or until the quiche is golden brown and just set – you want there to be a slight but definite wobble.

Tortilla Benidorm Style

There are versions of this classic omelette all over Spain, and when I was filming *Benidorm* it was regularly on the menu. This tortilla is perfect with a crisp green salad.

Serves 4

450g potatoes, peeled and cut into large chunks
2 tablespoons olive oil
1 Spanish onion, peeled and sliced
3 garlic cloves, peeled and crushed
8 eggs
Sea salt and freshly ground black pepper
3 tablespoons water
Small handful of torn basil leaves or chopped flat-leaf parsley leaves

Parboil the potatoes for 12 minutes, then drain and leave to cool. Once cool, cut the chunks into small cubes and set aside.

Heat the oil in a frying pan, add the onion and garlic and fry gently for about 8 minutes until soft. Remove from the pan and set aside. Add the potatoes to the frying pan and stir-fry for about 5 minutes before returning the onion and garlic to the pan.

Crack the eggs into a bowl and whisk them with some salt and pepper and the water. Pour this mixture over the potatoes and onion in the pan, ensuring the eggs cover the base of the pan. Cook for 5 minutes over a medium heat, then reduce the heat to as low as it will go and cook for another 10 minutes until the eggs are set.

Meanwhile, preheat the grill to a high setting. After the stove-top cooking time has elapsed, brown the top of the omelette under the grill.

Scatter some torn basil or chopped parsley over the top. (A sprinkling of grated Parmesan and a few toasted pine nuts would be good, too, though that might make it Italian rather than Spanish!) Serve immediately.

Newkie Brown Welsh Rarebit

Cheese on toast is delicious, but Welsh rarebit's even better. Use any well-flavoured hard cheese – I usually go for a Manchego. You wouldn't have found much of it in Newcastle or Nottingham when I was a child, but it's perfect for this classic dish. And if you're not a purist you could even add baked beans to the cheese mixture. I've always loved baked beans so I often do. They were all I would eat day and night from when I was about nine until I was twelve or so. Mum used to say I would look like one eventually. She's probably right!

Serves 2

1 teaspoon English mustard powder
3 tablespoons Newcastle Brown Ale
30g butter
Worcestershire sauce
175g mature hard cheese, grated

Sea salt and freshly ground black
  pepper
2 slices of good bread (Irish soda
  bread is nice in this dish)
2 egg yolks

Preheat the grill to its highest setting.

Mix the mustard powder with a little of the ale in the bottom of a small pan to make a paste.

Stir in the remaining beer, the butter and about 1 teaspoon Worcestershire sauce (you can always add more later, if you like). Heat gently until the butter has melted. Add the cheese and some salt and pepper and, again, stir until the cheese has melted, but don't let the mixture boil.

Once smooth, taste to check the seasoning, take the pan off the heat and allow the mixture to cool a little, but not too much. You don't want it to solidify.

Toast the bread lightly on both sides. Place the slices on a baking sheet.

Beat the egg yolks into the cheese mixture, then spoon it onto the toast. Place under a hot grill until the topping is bubbling and golden.

Sexy Tomato and Brie Pizza

Ripe, oozing Brie is such a sexy cheese. It's delicious with almost anything, but this pizza is particularly good.

Serves 4

Cornmeal, for dusting
1 x 7g sachet dried yeast
1 teaspoon granulated sugar
240ml warm water
375g plain flour, plus extra for
  dusting
1 teaspoon salt
2 tablespoons olive oil, plus
  extra for greasing
200g Brie, sliced

For the tomato topping
1½ tablespoons olive oil
2 teaspoons honey
2 garlic cloves, peeled and
  finely chopped
½ tablespoon balsamic vinegar
1 teaspoon soft light brown sugar
Sea salt and freshly
  ground black pepper
4 beef tomatoes, sliced
Handful of basil leaves, torn

Preheat the oven to 220°C/fan 200°C/gas mark 7. Lightly grease a 33cm pizza pan and dust it with cornmeal.

Make the tomato topping. Mix the olive oil, honey, garlic, balsamic vinegar, brown sugar and some salt and pepper. Put the tomatoes in a shallow bowl and pour the dressing over them. Throw the basil into the bowl, then turn the ingredients gently to mix. Leave the topping to marinate while you make the pizza dough.

Dissolve the yeast and sugar in the warm water (it should be no more than hand hot) in a bowl. Allow the mixture to stand for about 10 minutes until it is creamy.

Stir the flour, salt and oil into the bowl and beat until the mixture is smooth. Cover with a damp cloth and leave to rest in a warm place for 1 hour until doubled in size.

Turn out the dough on a lightly floured surface and roll it out into a round. The dough is very flexible, so you can easily manipulate it into shape. Transfer the dough to the prepared pizza pan. Spread over the tomato topping and lay over the slices of cheese. Bake for 15–20 minutes.

Coffee Mornings and Afternoon Delights

Victorian ladies would get up, have early morning tea, bathe, dress, have breakfast, then, later, a very light luncheon, after which they would change into something more comfortable (i.e. get out of their corsets). Then, in the afternoon, they would accept gentlemen callers for a bit of afternoon delight – a fondant fancy, perhaps! Now, we get up, take the kids to school with our coat on over our pyjamas, down a cappuccino, then get cracking with our busy day – no time for lunch – and our afternoon delights are playgroup or the ironing.

Afternoon delights are sexy, indulgent and necessary. Food is an aphrodisiac. It makes you feel good. My first proper boyfriend, Arthur, would pick me up in a yellow E-type Jag and we'd spend afternoons out, indulging in cream teas, toasted pikelets and sherbet fountains – heady days! We enjoyed every second, no matter what the weather.

So come on, let's all have some hot buttered pikelets again! We deserve them …

Lovely Lemon Sherbet Cakes

Sherbet dips (also known as Sherbet Fountains) are my absolute favourite – that little piece of liquorice makes life wonderful! You may say I need to get out more and you're right … but bring on the liquorice dipping. My addiction to these gorgeous sweets is rolled into cake heaven in this recipe. Yum!

Makes 12

120g self-raising flour
145g golden caster sugar
40g butter
Grated zest of 2 lemons
120ml full-fat milk
1 large egg
About 3 packets of Barratt's
    Sherbet Fountain

For the lemon curd
Grated zest and juice of
    4 unwaxed lemons
200g unrefined caster sugar
100g unsalted butter, cut into cubes
3 free range eggs and 1 free range
    egg yolk

First make the lemon curd. Put the lemon zest and juice, sugar and butter into a heat-proof bowl set over a pan of simmering water, ensuring the base of the bowl isn't sitting in the water. Stir the mixture every now and then until all the butter is melted.

Lightly whisk the eggs and egg yolk and stir them into the lemon mixture. Whisk until all the ingredients are combined. Leave to cook over the simmering water for 10–15 minutes, stirring intermittently, until the mixture is thick enough to coat the back of a spoon. Take the lemon curd off the heat and set aside. Once cool, spoon it into sterilised jars, seal and store in the fridge.

Now make the cakes. Preheat the oven to 180°C/fan 160°C/gas mark 4. Line a 12-hole muffin tin with cupcake cases.

Tip the flour, sugar, butter and lemon zest into a food processor and blitz on a slow speed for about 1 minute until you have a sandy consistency. Gradually pour in half the milk and beat. It'll seem a little messy, but don't worry about it.

In a separate bowl, whisk the remaining milk with the egg and pour this mixture into the batter. Mix for a couple of minutes until the batter is smooth.

Divide the batter between the cases and bake for 15–20 minutes. The cakes should be nicely golden brown and bounce back if you press them with your finger. Put the cakes on a wire rack and leave to cool. »

» Once the cakes are cool, cut a neat hole in the middle of each one with a small sharp knife. Fill each hole with a dollop of lemon curd. Sprinkle over some sherbet from the Sherbet Fountain packets. Cut the liquorice sticks into smaller pieces so you have 1 to pop onto each cake.

The Best Birthday Cake

Every nana should have a birthday cake in their repertoire. Shop-bought ones are all very well, but homemade is always better! This cake is so straightforward to make – it's filled with jam and buttercream and topped with more buttercream. The kids will love it. And you can jazz up this versatile recipe in any way you like. For example, turn it into a chocolate cake with a couple of tablespoonfuls of cocoa in both the cake mix and the icing, or make it a St Clement's cake by adding the grated zest of a lemon and an orange and a tablespoonful of the juice of each to both mixtures. And it doesn't have to be a plain round cake either – you can buy or even hire cake tins in amazing shapes these days. When Keeley was little, you had to get very creative with your sponge to make a princess cake or a train. Not so now. And you can buy all kinds of ready-rolled icing if you don't want to make your own. The important thing for kids is to really go to town with the decorations – sprinkles, silver balls, toasted coconut, flaked almonds and even little icing figures can be found easily in most supermarkets. For a teenager or a grown-up, you could keep the cake chic and simple with just a dusting of icing sugar and a single candle!

Serves 6

225g self-raising flour
1 teaspoon baking powder
4 large eggs
225g caster sugar
225g butter, softened, plus extra for greasing
½ teaspoon vanilla extract

2 tablespoons milk (if needed)
3 tablespoons strawberry jam

For the buttercream
175g butter, softened
1 teaspoon vanilla extract
450g icing sugar

Preheat the oven to 170°C/fan 150°C/gas mark 3½. Grease 2 x 20cm sandwich tins and line them with non-stick baking paper.

Sift the flour and the baking powder into a large mixing bowl. Add the eggs, sugar, butter and vanilla extract. Mix with a hand-held electric mixer or in an electric stand mixer until you have a smooth batter. It will only take a minute or 2. The mixture should drop off a spoon easily if you tap the spoon on the edge of the bowl. If it's too stiff, add a drop of water or milk to loosen it and mix again.

Divide the cake mixture equally between the 2 prepared tins, then knock them on the kitchen counter to get rid of any air bubbles. Put the tins in the centre of the oven and bake for 25–30 minutes – but don't peek or the sponges will sink. After 25 minutes, test by touching the centre of each sponge with a finger. If it springs back, it's ready.

Remove the cakes from the oven and leave to cool in the tins for 10 minutes. Then turn them out onto a cooling rack and leave to cool completely.

While the sponges cool, make the buttercream. Beat the butter, vanilla extract and icing sugar together in a bowl until light and fluffy. (If you want to colour the buttercream, add food colouring at this point and beat again.)

When the cakes are completely cool, place 1 of the sponges on a cake plate. Spread the jam over the top, then cover this with half the buttercream. Top with the other cake and cover it with the remaining buttercream. You can cover the sides, too, if you've got enough buttercream. Decorate further, if you would like to, then serve!

Singing Hinnies

These griddle scones are traditional in the North East, where 'hinny' is a term of endearment. My dad always used to call me Hinny. The rest of the name for this recipe comes from the fact that they 'sing' and sizzle in the pan.

Makes 8–12

225g plain flour, plus extra for dusting
Pinch of salt
1 teaspoon baking powder
50g butter, plus extra for greasing
25g lard
25g sugar
75g currants or sultanas
6–8 tablespoons milk
Butter, cheese and/or jam, to serve

Sift the flour, salt and baking powder together into a bowl. Rub in the butter and lard till the mixture resembles fine breadcrumbs.

Stir in the sugar and fruit. Gradually add the milk and mix to a stiff dough – you might not need all of the milk.

Roll the dough into a ball, then turn it out onto a lightly floured surface and flatten it into a round cake that's 1cm thick.

Lightly grease a frying pan or griddle and heat it over a medium-low heat. Place the hinny on it. Prick the top lightly with a fork and cook for 15–20 minutes, turning once, until it's golden brown on both sides.

Serve hot, cut into wedges, with butter and cheese and/or jam – in any combination you like.

Beautiful Bara Brith

My brother Brett has a tea shop in Llandudno called Characters, and he introduced me to bara brith, or speckled bread. It's a traditional Welsh fruit loaf and, in the past, it was very much a celebratory bread, baked at Christmas and for St David's Day. Now it's eaten all year round, toasted, with cheese, or just lashings of butter; whichever way, you'll have more than one piece.

Makes 1 x 900g loaf

110g currants
110g raisins
150g soft dark brown sugar
190ml strong hot tea
Butter, for greasing
200g self-raising flour
1 egg, beaten

Soak the fruit and sugar in the tea overnight.

Next day, preheat the oven to 150°C/fan 130°C/gas mark 2. Grease a 900g loaf tin and line it with non-stick baking paper.

Add half the flour to the soaked fruit and mix well. Add the beaten egg and remaining flour and mix well.

Spread the mixture in the prepared tin. Bake for about 1½ hours or until a skewer inserted into the middle comes out clean. Remove from the tin and cool on a wire rack.

Fabulous Figgy Flapjacks

We all remember figgy biscuits, don't we? But you don't really see them much these days. I suppose they don't have sex appeal – unlike, say, a chocolate HobNob or these wonderful flapjacks, which are gooey and sticky and very delicious!

Makes 20

175g butter, plus extra for greasing
125g golden caster sugar
75g golden syrup, plus extra for drizzling
200g rolled oats
100g sultanas
15 dried apricots, chopped
2 tablespoons ground almonds
10 dried figs, quartered

Preheat the oven to 180°C/fan 160°C/gas mark 4. Grease a 23 x 30cm baking tray and line it with non-stick baking paper.

Melt the butter, sugar and syrup in a saucepan. When melted, add the oats, sultanas, chopped apricots and ground almonds and stir well.

Transfer the mixture to the prepared baking tray and press it firmly into the tin. Place the figs on top, drizzle with a little syrup, then bake for 15–20 minutes until the edges are nicely browned.

Remove the tray from the oven and leave the flapjack in the tin until almost cool. Cut into 20 squares before the flapjack is completely cold.

Very Cherry Scones

There's nothing like a good scone, is there? Piled high with jam and cream, they make a wonderful teatime treat. These scones, made using glacé cherries, are a variant on the traditional scone with raisins, and they're fabulous!

Makes 12

240g self-raising flour, plus extra for dusting
2 teaspoons baking powder
60g butter, plus extra for greasing
2 tablespoons caster sugar
1 egg, lightly beaten
100ml milk
100g glacé cherries, quartered

To serve
Clotted cream or whipped double cream
Jam (any flavour you wish)

Preheat the oven to 230°C/fan 210°C/gas mark 8. Grease a baking sheet.

Put the flour and baking powder in a mixing bowl and rub in the butter. Stir in the sugar, then add the egg, the milk and the cherries. Stir the mixture to form a soft dough.

Turn out the scone dough onto a floured board and knead for a moment or 2, but don't overdo it.

Roll out the dough to a thickness of about 1cm. Use a 5cm round cutter to cut out 12 circles. Place these on the prepared baking sheet and bake in the centre of the oven for 10–12 minutes until well risen and golden. Leave to cool on a wire rack, then serve with cream and jam.

Perky Pikelets

Depending on where you were born, you are either a pikelet or a crumpet person, just as you might say either cob or bun for a bread roll. In Nottingham, we were definitely pikelet people! When I was little we used to toast these in front of the fire with toasting forks and have them with lashings of butter. This would not be considered healthy these days, but once in a while won't hurt!

Makes 24

1 egg
4 tablespoons caster sugar
210ml milk
Sea salt
200g plain flour
1 teaspoon baking powder
30g butter, melted
Sunflower oil, for greasing
Butter, honey, jam, cream, crème fraîche, fruit and/or cheese, to serve

Whisk together the egg, sugar, milk and salt in a medium-sized bowl. Sift the flour and baking powder into a separate bowl. Pour the butter and the egg mixture into the flour. Stir quickly until the dry ingredients are moist but still a bit lumpy – do not overmix.

Heat a greased griddle or a heavy-based frying pan over a medium heat. Drop dessertspoonfuls of the mixture from the tip of the spoon into the pan, leaving plenty of space between each pikelet so you can move them about while they cook. Cook over a medium heat (too little heat makes heavy, pale pikelets; too much, and they're liable to burn) and turn them over as soon as bubbles appear on the surface. They should be nicely golden on both sides.

Serve the pikelets hot with butter, honey, jam, sliced bananas, blackberries, cream, crème fraîche and pomegranate seeds, or – you know what I'm going to say – cheese!

Chocolate-Dipped Coconut Macaroons

Olly and Molly love making these macaroons, especially dipping the macaroons into the melted chocolate. Well, who wouldn't? It can be very messy, in a chocolate-covered fingers sort of way, but it's the best fun in the world.

Makes 24

Butter, for greasing
3 egg whites
250g caster sugar
½ teaspoon coconut essence
1 tablespoon grated lemon zest
2 tablespoons cornflour, sifted
300g desiccated coconut
3 tablespoons shredded coconut, for sprinkling
60g dark chocolate, chopped

Preheat the oven to 160°C/fan 140°C/gas mark 3. Grease 2 baking sheets and line them with non-stick baking paper.

Place the egg whites in a dry bowl and, using a hand-held electric mixer or an electric stand mixer, beat them until they form stiff peaks. Add the sugar gradually, beating constantly until the mixture is thick and glossy and all the sugar has been incorporated.

Add the coconut essence and lemon zest and beat until combined. Fold the sifted cornflour and desiccated coconut into the mixture with a metal spoon.

Drop 1–2 level teaspoonfuls of the macaroon mixture onto the prepared baking sheets, spacing them about 3cm apart. Sprinkle with shredded coconut and bake for 15–20 minutes or until the macaroons are golden. Transfer to a cooling rack.

Melt the chocolate in a heat-proof bowl set over a pan of simmering water, ensuring the base of the bowl isn't sitting in the water. Dip the cooled macaroons sideways into the melted chocolate to completely coat one-half and return to the wire rack to set.

Gorgeous Gingerbread

As long as your gingerbread is moist, that's all that matters. I would have sliced gingerbread with a strong cheese or soft Brie. Normal people, on the other hand, would have it plain, or with a nice cup of tea. With a coulis, it's transformed into a lovely pudding. Come to think of it, I'd probably have the cheese and the coulis – and the Chantilly cream topping, too!

Serves 8

115g butter
2 tablespoons treacle
1 tablespoon golden syrup
240ml milk
300g plain flour
175g soft dark brown sugar
1 teaspoon ground ginger
Pinch of salt
1 egg, beaten
1 teaspoon bicarbonate of soda
1 teaspoon baking powder
½ teaspoon mixed spice
240ml boiling water

For the coulis

2 medium mangoes,
   peeled and chopped
30g stem ginger
Juice of 1 lime

For the Chantilly cream

1–2 tablespoons caster sugar
240ml double or whipping cream,
   (with at least 35 per cent
   butterfat content)
¼ teaspoon vanilla extract

For the orange-ginger frosting (optional)

4 tablespoons unsalted butter
225g cream cheese
225g icing sugar
Grated zest of 1 orange
2 teaspoons finely grated
   fresh root ginger
Pinch of salt

Preheat the oven to 180°C/fan 160°C/gas mark 4. Line a 450g loaf tin with non-stick baking paper.

To make the gingerbread, melt the butter, treacle and golden syrup in the milk in a saucepan set over a gentle heat. Mix the flour, sugar, ground ginger and salt in a bowl, then add the buttery syrup and the beaten egg and mix well.

Dissolve the bicarb, baking powder and mixed spice in the boiling water, then add this to the mixture, stirring to incorporate. Pour the mixture into the prepared tin and bake for 30–40 minutes until risen and nicely firm. Remember – it should be moist, so don't overcook! Leave it to cool in the tin. »

» While the gingerbread is in the oven, make the coulis. In a food processor or blender, purée the mango, ginger and lime juice until smooth. Set aside in the fridge. (It will keep, covered and refrigerated, for up to a week.)

When the gingerbread has cooled completely, make the Chantilly cream. Make sure everything is really cold – not just the cream, but the bowl and whisk, too. You could even pop the bowl in the freezer for a few minutes beforehand. Add 1 tablespoon of the sugar to the cream and vanilla extract in your chilled bowl and start to whip, very gently at first – especially if you're using a hand-held electric mixer. If you are, switch to a hand whisk once it starts to thicken and continue to beat until the cream has reached the soft peak stage. Taste for sweetness and add more sugar if you'd like it sweeter. That's it!

Slice the gingerbread into 8 portions. Pile the Chantilly cream on top of the gingerbread (or serve it in dollops alongside), spoon over a generous helping of the coulis and serve.

If you prefer to use an orange-ginger frosting instead of the cream, you can make that while the cake is baking, too. Place the butter into the bowl of an electric stand mixer with a paddle attachment (or use a food processor) and beat on medium-high speed for about 2 minutes until fluffy. Add the cream cheese and sugar, beat well for 2 minutes, then add the orange zest, grated ginger and salt and beat for a further 5 minutes. Pile on top of the cooled, sliced gingerbread and serve with the coulis.

Golden Toffee Banana Bread

Those four words make me smile and this sweet bread is comfy, yummy and very happy-making. OK, it's not a slimming option, but who's looking?! Go for it and enjoy.

Makes 1 x 450g loaf

250g plain flour
1 teaspoon baking powder
Pinch of sea salt
115g butter, plus extra for greasing
115g soft dark brown sugar
2 eggs, beaten
750g bananas, peeled and mashed with a fork
100g toffees, cut into small pieces

Preheat the oven to 180°C/fan 160°C/gas mark 4. Lightly grease a 450g loaf tin.

Sift the flour, baking powder and salt into a bowl. In a separate bowl, cream together the butter and brown sugar. Stir in the eggs and the mashed bananas and mix well to combine.

Stir the banana mixture into the flour and mix thoroughly. Stir in the toffee pieces, keeping some back for the topping. Pour the mixture into the prepared loaf tin and bake for about 1 hour.

About 5 minutes before you take the banana bread out of the oven, sprinkle over the remaining pieces of toffee. Test the bread with a knife or skewer. If it comes out clean, it's done. Remove the bread from the oven and turn out onto a cooling rack.

Serve the bread in slices, as it is, with butter or – of course – cheese!

Moreish Marshmallow and Chocolate Cheesecake

I'm a bit addicted to marshmallows. It began with a boyfriend I had when I was fourteen who looked like Paul McCartney – well, they all did then! When he called for me he always brought a bag of marshmallows, but after a few dates he dumped me. Still, he inspired this unusual cheesecake, created in the hope that it would win me a new PMcC lookalike … It never did, but I still cherish this dish.

Serves 6–8

175g digestive biscuits or HobNobs, crushed

85g butter, melted

580g cream cheese

120g caster sugar

1 teaspoon vanilla extract

3 eggs, beaten

2 egg yolks

115g tiny marshmallows

For the chocolate ganache topping

300ml double cream

150g dark chocolate, broken into pieces

Preheat the oven to 180°C/fan 160°C/gas mark 4.

Mix the crushed biscuits with the melted butter and press the mixture into the base of a 23cm springform cake tin. Chill for 30 minutes or until firm. Wrap the outside of the tin with kitchen foil.

To make the filling, mix the cream cheese, sugar and vanilla extract in a bowl. Beat in the eggs and egg yolks, then gently fold in the marshmallows. Spoon the mixture into the tin over the biscuit base and level off the top.

Place the cake tin in a roasting tin that's half-full of boiling water. Bake for 50 minutes. Remove the tin from the oven and leave the cheesecake to cool, then chill for 2–3 hours or until firm.

Make the topping. Bring the cream up to the boil, but don't let it actually boil. Take the pan off the heat and stir in the chocolate. Stir until the mixture is smooth and the chocolate has melted. Leave to cool for 10 minutes, then pour it over the cheesecake and chill in the tin until the chocolate ganache has set.

Deliciously Wicked Devil's Food Cake

This is a gorgeously rich chocolate cake, devilishly designed to tempt you and anyone else who is lucky enough to share it with you. So make sure you serve it in generous slices – with ice cream, if you like! Being wicked is the name of the game here …

Serves 6–8

50g cocoa
100g soft dark brown sugar
250ml boiling water
125g butter, softened, plus
    extra for greasing
125g caster sugar
1 teaspoon vanilla extract
2 eggs

225g plain flour
1 teaspoon baking powder

For the icing
125ml water
30g soft dark brown sugar
175g butter, cubed
300g dark chocolate, chopped

Preheat the oven to 180°C/fan 160°C/gas mark 4. Grease and line 2 x 20cm sandwich tins.

Dissolve the cocoa and dark brown sugar in a bowl with the boiling water. Whisk the mixture well to get rid of any lumps, then set aside.

Cream the butter and caster sugar in a separate bowl until fluffy. Add the vanilla extract, then beat in the eggs, 1 at a time. Fold in the flour and baking powder. Finally, add the cocoa mixture and mix thoroughly.

Divide the batter equally between the 2 prepared tins and bake for about 30 minutes or until a skewer inserted into each cake comes out clean. Leave the cakes to cool in the tins for 10 minutes, then turn them out onto a wire rack to cool.

While the cakes are in the oven, make the icing. Put the water, brown sugar and butter into a pan and melt the mixture over a low heat. When it's thoroughly melted, take the pan off the heat and stir in the chopped chocolate. Leave for a minute or 2 without stirring, then whisk it all together until the mixture is really smooth and shiny. Set aside for an hour or until the cakes are completely cool.

Place 1 of the cakes on a cake plate, spread the top with about one-third of the icing, then top it with the other cake. Spread the remaining icing over the top and sides, and your cake is ready to serve.

Nana's Boozy Fruit Cake

This is partly my nana's recipe and partly my dad's. Nana covered the cake in marzipan and royal icing. Dad, once he'd made the cake, would feed it a tablespoonful of brandy every day for six months, then ice it for Christmas. Everyone wanted one of his cakes and he'd take orders in January for the following Christmas. Even the smallest piece warms the cockles of your heart.

Makes 1 x 23cm cake

175g raisins
350g glacé cherries, halved
500g currants
250g sultanas
150ml brandy (or use sherry, if you prefer)
Grated zest of 2 oranges
250g butter, softened, plus extra for greasing

250g soft dark brown sugar
4 eggs
1 tablespoon treacle
75g blanched almonds, coarsely chopped
250g plain flour
1½ teaspoons mixed spice

Put all the dried fruit into a large mixing bowl and pour over the brandy. Stir in the orange zest, cover with cling film and leave to soak overnight.

Next day, preheat the oven to 140°C/fan 120°C/gas mark 1. Grease and line a deep 23cm cake tin.

Put the butter, sugar, eggs, treacle and almonds into a very large bowl and beat well – if you've got an electric stand mixer, use it! If not, use a hand-held electric mixer or a wooden spoon and a lot of elbow grease! Fold in the flour and mixed spice and mix well. Stir in the soaked fruit along with any remaining brandy. Pour the mixture into the prepared cake tin and level off the surface.

Bake in the centre of the oven for 4–4½ hours or until the cake is firm to the touch and is a rich golden brown. Check it after 2 hours – if it already has a good colour, cover it with kitchen foil to prevent it from burning during cooking. Check the cake with a skewer – if it comes out clean, it is done. Leave it to cool in the tin for ½ hour, then turn it out onto a rack to cool completely.

Nana's Pantry

As a child, the smell of my nana's pantry was all I needed to make me feel happy, needed and reassured. When I was at drama school, I lived with the love of my life – or so I thought at the time! We had a very small and grubby flat in a back street in London. I wanted to play wife at the age of eighteen, so I tried to emulate my nana. I remembered her standing over the stove in her kitchen making jam, so I decided that's what I would make. I went out and begged and stole pots and pans and ingredients. I didn't have a clue what I was doing and had no phone to ring my nana, so I made it up. Unfortunately, I left the boiling jam mix on the stove on a high flame for too long … Not only did the old pan start to burn through the bottom, but the jam exploded all over the tiny little kitchen and I had to cover myself with a blanket to get to the stove to turn the gas off.

So learn from my lesson and follow the recipe. And use good pans that are not from 1947! The recipes in this chapter are not difficult to make when you know how …

Rhubarb and Ginger Jam

Who grows rhubarb in their garden any more? Hardly anyone, but when I was a child, we all did. On a hot summer's day, we pulled the long red sticks straight out of the ground and dipped them in white sugar – it was just heaven. Today, people might go all health and safety and say it was unhygienic. But it's not, it's perfectly safe and it's fantastic raw. Rhubarb also makes the most wonderful jam. And when you mix this garden jewel with ginger … well, need I say more?

Makes enough to fill 3 x 200g jars

600g rhubarb, sliced into small pieces
500g jam sugar with added pectin
2 tablespoons syrup from a jar of stem ginger
4 pieces of stem ginger, chopped

Put the rhubarb pieces in a large pan. Add the sugar, mix thoroughly and cover. Set aside for a few hours or leave overnight. The sugar draws the juice out of the rhubarb, which helps it to keep its shape when you cook it.

Bring the rhubarb and its juice to the boil, then add the ginger syrup. Boil rapidly for 5 minutes or until setting point is reached. Test for this by putting a bit of the jam on a saucer that has been in the freezer. Let it cool slightly, then push it with a finger to see if it wrinkles. If it does, it has reached setting point. If it doesn't, continue to boil until it does.

Once the jam has passed the crinkle test, take it off the heat and stir in the stem ginger.

Leave the jam to cool a little, then transfer it into sterilised jars and seal immediately. Store this jam for up to 6 months. Consume within 1 month once opened.

Super Strawberry Jam

We all used to go strawberry and blackberry picking with our nanas, didn't we? Of course, we'd eat most of them, but the ones that did make it home were magically transformed into a rich, shining jam, bottled and carefully labelled.

Makes enough to fill 4 x 200g jars

1kg strawberries, hulled
1kg jam sugar with added pectin
Juice of 1 large lemon, plus the pips (tied in a scrap of muslin)
Knob of butter

Put the whole strawberries, jam sugar, lemon juice and the pips in their little bag into a large, wide saucepan. Heat the mixture gently, stirring from time to time, until the sugar is completely dissolved, then bring to the boil. Boil rapidly for about 5–6 minutes until setting point (see page 78) is reached.

Remove the pan from the heat and skim off any scum from the surface with a metal spoon. Add the knob of butter and stir (this will help disperse any remaining scum). Leave the jam to cool for at least 30 minutes. Stir well, then ladle the jam into sterilised jars. Store this jam for up to 6 months. Consume within 1 month once opened.

Orange Chutney

This chutney makes a lovely present, not just on festive occasions but at any time. Serve with strong cheese, crackers or chunky bread and a glass of wine or a rich port. Put your feet up by the fire as well and life is good.

Makes enough to fill 3 x 200g jars

1 large onion, peeled
8 cloves
1 tablespoon olive oil
1 teaspoon black mustard seeds
2 Bramley apples, peeled and chopped
5 oranges, peeled, segmented and chopped
Finely chopped zest of 1 orange
150g soft light brown sugar
300ml cider vinegar

Slice off the root end of the onion, stud it with cloves and set aside. Finely chop the rest of the onion.

Heat the oil in a large saucepan and gently sweat the chopped onion until softened and starting to caramelise. Add the mustard seeds and apple and sweat gently for a further 5 minutes.

Add the orange and orange zest, the clove-studded onion, the sugar and the vinegar. Bring to the boil, then simmer gently for 40–50 minutes, by which time the mixture should be thick but not too dry.

Spoon the warm chutney into sterilised jars, cover with lids and allow it to cool. Store this chutney for up to 6 months. Refrigerate and consume within 1 month once opened.

Red Onion Marmalade

I love red onions – raw in salad, fried with a hotdog, or folded into a jacket potato, they are so much more desirable than their white onion sisters. In this marmalade they are, in the words of Janette Krankie, 'Fan-Dabi-Dozi'. This goes with everything: cheese, ham, pâté, you name it. A dollop on top of a salad is all you need.

Makes enough to fill 3 x 200g jars

2 tablespoons extra-virgin olive oil
1kg red onions, peeled, halved and sliced
Sea salt and freshly ground black pepper
150ml red wine
3 tablespoons balsamic vinegar
3 tablespoons white wine vinegar
6 tablespoons light soft brown sugar

Heat the oil in a preserving pan or a large, heavy stainless steel pan. Add the onions and a pinch each of salt and pepper. Cook over a medium-low heat, stirring occasionally, for about 30 minutes until the onions soften and become translucent. Don't let them burn, and take your time – slow cooking is essential at this point as this is how the delicious caramel flavour is developed.

Raise the heat a little, add the wine and vinegars and stir to combine. Bring the mixture to the boil, then reduce the heat, stir in the sugar and cook over a low heat, still stirring from time to time, for another 30–40 minutes or until most of the liquid has evaporated.

Remove the pan from the heat. Taste and adjust the seasoning as necessary, but remember that the flavours will mature with time.

Spoon the marmalade into warm sterilised jars with non-metallic or vinegar-proof lids, ensuring there are no air pockets. Cover with waxed paper discs, seal and label. Store in a cool dark place for 1 month to mature.

Store this marmalade for up to 6 months. Refrigerate and consume within 1 month once opened.

Teatime with
the Kids

We all love kids' food, don't we? It's real comfort food and always conjures up such wonderful memories. Now as a nana, I'm back amongst all those yummy things again: fish-finger sandwiches, chicken and chips in a basket, peanut butter, Wagon Wheels, lashings of ginger beer … I used to love Enid Blyton's Famous Five books, and in the summer one of my favourite things to do with the kids is to pack up an old-fashioned picnic, in a proper hamper with all the plates and knives and forks attached. When I was filming *The Russ Abbot Show* we did a hysterical Famous Five spoof. As with all the sketches in Russ's shows it was mad and silly – Russ and I were the Famous Two trying to solve a crime in Devon in the 1950s. We had the picnic hamper, and we literally had lashings of ginger beer, iced buns, Victoria sponge, even cucumber sandwiches and, of course, Wagon Wheels. It was a lovely hot summer and we filmed for four weeks. It was glorious to be a kid again. Now, as a nana, I want to give my grandchildren glorious memories of happy times with the biggest kid of them all – me!

Share the recipes in this chapter with your children, grandchildren, or with all the other grown-up children you know.

Scrummy Sweetcorn Pancakes

These pancakes are always well received in my home, either on their own with lashings of tomato ketchup as a filling after-school snack, or with bacon or sausages.

Serves 4

2 eggs
5 tablespoons milk
25g butter, melted
Pinch of salt
85g self-raising flour
340g can sweetcorn, drained
Sunflower oil, for shallow-frying

Whisk the eggs, milk, melted butter, salt and flour in a bowl until you have a smooth batter. Add the sweetcorn and mix well.

Heat a little oil in a frying pan and, when hot, drop in spoonfuls of the pancake batter. Fry for about 2–3 minutes on each side until the pancakes are cooked through and golden brown. Remove them from the pan, drain on kitchen paper and keep warm while you continue to cook more pancakes until all the mixture has been used.

Really Cheesy Macaroni Cheese

Crisp and crunchy on top, rich and creamy underneath, this macaroni cheese is so delicious – and all the calcium in the cheese helps kids grow strong bones. So it's good for them, too.

Serves 4

400g macaroni
Butter, for greasing

For the cheese sauce
50g butter
50g plain flour
450ml milk
85g Gruyère cheese, grated
60g Parmesan cheese, grated
150g mascarpone

For the topping
40g fresh breadcrumbs
30g Parmesan cheese, grated

Make the sauce first. Melt the butter in a saucepan set over a low heat, then mix in the flour. Stir until the mixture comes away from the sides of the pan, then very gradually incorporate the milk. Stir vigorously as you add the milk – you don't want any lumps. Cook over a low heat, stirring constantly, until the sauce has thickened. It should coat the back of the spoon. Stir in the cheeses and mix thoroughly until they melt into the sauce. Set aside.

Cook the pasta in a large pan of salted water. Meanwhile, preheat the grill to a high setting and grease a medium-sized oven-proof dish. Mix the fresh breadcrumbs with the Parmesan for the topping.

When the pasta is just al dente, mix it into the sauce. Pour the mixture into the prepared dish and scatter over the topping. Brown under the grill until crisp and bubbling. Serve immediately.

Pasta with Nana's Homemade Tomato Pesto

I came up with this pesto recipe years ago and it makes a lovely change from the usual version, made with basil, although the kids love that, too, of course.

Serves 4

400g pasta (choose shapes specially made for kids)

For the pesto
300g sundried tomatoes, chopped
150g black olives, stoned and chopped
4 tablespoons pine nuts, toasted
8 tablespoons olive oil
40g Parmesan cheese, grated
3 garlic cloves, peeled and crushed
Pinch of dried oregano
Sea salt and freshly ground black pepper

Put the sundried tomatoes, olives and pine nuts into the goblet of a blender with the olive oil. Blend until puréed – but don't make the mixture too smooth. Add the Parmesan, garlic, oregano and salt and pepper and give it a last blitz.

Cook the pasta according to the packet instructions in boiling salted water, or you can use chicken stock instead for a bit of extra flavour. Drain the pasta, return it to the pan, then mix in the pesto. Serve immediately.

Spaghetti and Meatballs

I've yet to meet a child who didn't love this dish. And kids love rolling the meatballs, too, so it's a good recipe to get them roped into.

Serves 6

3 tablespoons olive oil

½ onion, peeled and chopped

3 garlic cloves, peeled and chopped

1 large carrot, peeled and
    finely chopped

100g brown mushrooms, chopped

400g can Italian tomatoes

2 tablespoons chopped basil leaves

2 tablespoons chopped flat-leaf
    parsley leaves

1 tablespoon tomato purée

225g Italian sausages

450g minced beef

1 egg

25g breadcrumbs

50g grated Parmesan cheese,
    plus extra to serve

2 teaspoons sea salt

2 teaspoons pepper

90ml red wine

675g thin spaghetti
    (spaghettini)

Heat 2 tablespoons of the oil in a pan, add the onion and cook for 2 minutes over a medium heat. Add the garlic and cook for 1 minute, then add the carrots and half the mushrooms. Stir together well and pour in the tomatoes and 1 tablespoon each of the basil and parsley. If the tomatoes are too chunky, break them down with a potato masher. Cook gently for 5 minutes until the sauce has started to thicken. Add the tomato purée, reduce the heat to low and simmer, stirring occasionally, for about 30 minutes while you make the meatballs.

Squeeze the sausagemeat out of the casings into a bowl. Place the beef, remaining herbs and mushrooms, egg, breadcrumbs, half the Parmesan, and the salt and pepper into a bowl and mix the ingredients together by hand. Take a generous teaspoonful of the mixture and roll it into a ball. Repeat with the remaining mixture.

Heat a frying pan over a high heat, add the remaining oil and sear and brown the meatballs over a medium-high heat for about 2–3 minutes. Be careful not to overcrowd the pan; they don't like it. Once the meatballs are all nicely browned, remove them from the pan, add 2 tablespoons red wine to the pan and deglaze it.

Add the remaining wine to the tomato sauce, bring the sauce back up to the boil, then add the mixture from the deglazed pan, the remaining cheese and the meatballs. Taste to check the seasoning, adjusting it if necessary, and simmer for 35–40 minutes.

While the sauce simmers, fill a large pot with water and bring it to the boil for the spaghetti.

When boiling, add salt, then add the pasta and cook according to the packet instructions. When it's done, drain the pasta well then tip it into a large serving bowl. Cover with the meatballs and their sauce. Serve with extra grated Parmesan to sprinkle over each portion.

Tomatoey Sausage Rolls

I think these fuss-free sausage rolls should be served up at every picnic, but they're just as good for tea at home. You could use ready-rolled pastry, but the kids love having a go with the rolling pin!

Makes 16

250g puff pastry
Tomato ketchup

450g sausagemeat
Milk, for brushing

Preheat the oven to 200°C/fan 180°C/gas mark 6.

Roll out the puff pastry to roughly 30 x 36cm. Brush the pastry with some tomato ketchup.

Place a strip of sausagemeat along 1 long edge of the pastry, leaving a large enough section of pastry to fold over and cover the sausagemeat. Dampen the edge of the pastry with milk and roll it over the sausagemeat. Press down to seal the edges of the pastry.

Make diagonal cuts across the top of the roll, then cut it into roughly 16 individual rolls.

Place the rolls on a baking sheet and bake in the middle of the oven for 10–15 minutes until they are golden brown and cooked through.

Lemon Fish Fingers and Special Homemade Chips

Better than Birds Eye any day! Get the kids to peel the potatoes and cut them into chips. They can egg and flour the fish, too.

Serves 2

For the fish fingers
2 skinless haddock fillets
2 tablespoons plain flour
Sea salt and a very generous grinding of black pepper
Grated zest of 1 lemon
1 egg, beaten
Sunflower oil, for shallow-frying
Lemon wedges, to serve

For the chips
2 baking potatoes, peeled
2 tablespoons sunflower oil, plus extra for greasing

Preheat the oven to 200°C/fan 180°C/gas mark 6. Grease a baking tray.

Make the chips first. Cut the peeled potatoes into thin chips. Toss them in the oil in a mixing bowl, then spread them out on the prepared baking tray. Bake for 20–30 minutes until cooked through. Turn them over halfway through the cooking time so that they brown evenly.

While the chips are cooking, wash the fish fillets and pat them dry with kitchen paper. Cut each fillet into 7–8cm fingers.

Put the flour on a plate and season it with salt, pepper and lemon zest. Mix well. Coat the fish pieces with the seasoned flour, then dip them into the beaten egg. Now roll them in the flour again.

Heat the oil in a frying pan and shallow-fry the fish fingers over a medium heat for about 3 minutes on each side until crisp and golden.

Serve the fish fingers with a spritz of lemon and sea salt, with your homemade chips.

Chicken Pitta Pockets

These are a far cry from the take-away kebabs I used to eat in my RADA days! Much healthier, certainly – and a lot tastier, too. If you – or the kids – are keen on chilli, then add a good splash of hot sauce before you serve them.

Serves 4

1 tablespoon olive oil, plus extra for shallow-frying
Juice of ½ lemon
2 garlic cloves, peeled and crushed
Pinch of dried oregano
Sea salt and freshly ground black pepper
2 boneless, skinless chicken breasts, sliced into strips
¼ cucumber, peeled and coarsely chopped
3 tablespoons Greek yogurt
4 pitta breads
Handful of Cos or iceberg lettuce, shredded
2 tomatoes, quartered

Mix the olive oil, lemon juice, half the crushed garlic, the oregano and some salt and pepper in a bowl. Add the chicken strips and turn them in the mixture, then leave the bowl in the fridge for at least 30 minutes to allow the chicken to marinate.

Mix the cucumber, remaining crushed garlic and the yogurt together in a bowl and set aside.

Heat a splash of olive oil in a frying pan. Remove the chicken from the marinade and cook it over a medium-low heat until golden brown all over.

While the chicken is cooking, warm the pitta breads in a toaster or under a grill. Then cut a slit along 1 edge of each pitta bread and open it out. Stuff with lettuce and a dollop of the cucumber and yogurt mixture. Divide the chicken strips into 4 equal portions and add 1 portion to each pitta. Top with pieces of tomato, then serve immediately.

Spotty Doggie

Good old-fashioned steamed puddings seem to be a bit neglected these days, but this is an easy recipe for the kids to make and there's time for them to play out and work up an appetite while it's cooking. Most people know it as spotted dick, but we always call it spotty doggie.

Serves 6

325g plain flour, plus extra for dusting
2 teaspoons baking powder
Pinch of sea salt
60g caster sugar
150g currants
180g shredded suet
2 eggs, beaten
150ml milk (but you might need a tiny bit more)
Custard, to serve

Put a large pan of water on to boil.

Before you begin mixing, lay out a large square of muslin and dust it with flour. You'll see why in a minute.

Sift the flour into a large bowl with the baking powder and salt. Add the sugar, currants, suet, beaten eggs and milk and mix to form a stiffish dough. Turn out the mixture onto the prepared cloth and shape it into a ball with floured hands. Roll up the pudding cloth to encase the mixture, tie it up with kitchen string and boil it for 1½ hours.

Serve hot with homemade custard or a good-quality shop-bought one.

Iced Bun Family Tree

Get the children's imaginations going with these iced buns – they can represent themselves, Mummy and Daddy, and brothers and sisters, too. Creativity is the name of the game here. First you need to decide on the colours for the icing. Are you orange with pink stripes? Is Mummy red with white spots? And what about Daddy? But that's not all – you can also be really creative in what you use to make the faces. Try silver balls, hundreds and thousands, fruit and even veg; how about apple or cucumber smiles and grated carrot hair? And what about currants or slivers of radish for eyes? Use anything you like! The recipe makes 12 so you can have lots of variations.

Makes 12

Melted butter, for greasing
Sunflower oil, for brushing
350–450g plain flour, plus
    extra for dusting
35g full-cream milk powder
2 x 7g sachets easy blend dried yeast
½ teaspoon salt
115g caster sugar
55g sultanas
60g butter, melted
1 egg, lightly beaten

225ml warm water
1 egg yolk beaten with
    1 tablespoon water
Decorations of your
    choice (see above)

For the icing
140g icing sugar
2–3 teaspoons water
Food colourings of your choice

Brush 2 large baking sheets with melted butter or oil. Lightly oil a mixing bowl.

Put 350g of the flour into a large bowl with the milk powder, yeast, salt, sugar and sultanas. Mix thoroughly, then make a well in the centre of the mixture. Mix together the butter, egg and warm water and pour this into the well. Stir for 2–3 minutes. Mix in just enough of the remaining flour to make a dough.

Turn out the dough onto a lightly floured surface and knead for 10 minutes or until smooth and elastic. Place the dough into the prepared bowl and brush the surface with oil. Cover with cling film and leave in a warm place to rise for about 1 hour.

Punch the dough a few times with your fist (this is very therapeutic for the grown-ups and great fun for the kids), then knead it for 1 more minute. Divide »

» the dough into 12 pieces and shape these into round buns – they don't all have to be the same shape, so let the kids choose! Place them onto the prepared baking sheets, spacing them 5cm apart. Cover with cling film and leave in a warm place for 20 minutes until risen.

Preheat the oven to 180°C/fan 160°C/gas mark 4.

Brush the dough pieces well with the egg yolk and water mixture, then bake for 20 minutes until the buns are well risen and pale golden brown. Leave to cool on a wire rack.

When the buns have cooled, make the icing. This is where the fun really starts. Mix the icing sugar with just enough of the water to create a smooth mixture. Now decide on the colours you wish to use and divide up the icing into the amounts you need, putting each of these into a separate bowl. Now add just enough food colouring to each portion to create the colour you want. Stir thoroughly and off you go – ice the buns and make your faces! Use a palette knife to smooth the icing over the top of the buns, then add your chosen decorations to make the faces. The kids will have a field day.

Nutty Banana Milkshake

All kids love thick, creamy, ice-cold milkshakes. Adding banana means you're not only giving them a sweet treat, but getting some fruit inside them, too!

Serves 2

2 large scoops of chocolate ice cream
2 bananas
2 tablespoons smooth peanut butter
250ml milk

Whizz all ingredients in a blender, adding more or less milk depending on how thick you like your milkshake. Pour the mixture into 2 tall glasses and serve with a straw.

Proper Tiffin

You can add other goodies to this recipe – chopped glacé cherries or chopped walnuts, for instance. This tiffin makes a great snack with a glass of cold milk or a milkshake.

Makes 20
110g butter
1 dessertspoon caster sugar
1 tablespoon golden syrup
50g sultanas
2 tablespoons drinking chocolate
175g digestive biscuits, crushed
175g chocolate, chopped

Melt the butter in a pan. Take the pan off the heat, add all the other ingredients except the chocolate and mix well.

Spread the mixture into a 23 x 30cm Swiss roll tin and leave to set.

When the mixture is cold, melt the chocolate in a heat-proof bowl set over a pan of simmering water, ensuring the base of the bowl isn't sitting in the water.

Once the chocolate has melted, pour it over the mixture in the Swiss roll tin and ensure the entire lower layer is covered in melted chocolate. Leave to set, then cut into 20 squares.

Peanut Butter Toffee Ice Cream

You need an ice cream maker for this recipe – you can make it without, but it's a bit of a palaver. Make sure you put the bowl of the ice cream maker in the freezer overnight before churning – unless you've got one of those really fancy ones which doesn't need it. And have lots of ice cubes ready – you'll see why! Of course, you could skip the ice cream maker altogether and add the peanut butter and toffee to a very good shop-bought vanilla ice cream, but the kids love the process, although they do get very impatient. Perhaps do both?! The recipe is very versatile, too. You could add bits of broken cookies, or chocolate chips and almonds. There are lots of possibilities.

Serves 6–8

250ml double cream
300ml full-fat milk
115g golden caster sugar
1 vanilla pod
3 large free range egg yolks
2 tablespoons chunky peanut butter
2 tablespoons chopped soft toffees (about 6 toffees)

Put the cream and milk into a heavy-based pan and add half the sugar. Slit the vanilla pod down its length, scoop out the black seeds and add them to the cream. Cut the pod into 3 and add it to the pan, too.

Heat the cream and milk over a low heat, stirring occasionally, until nearly boiling. Take the pan off the heat and set aside for 30 minutes to allow the vanilla to infuse.

Put the egg yolks in a bowl with the remaining sugar and beat with a hand-held electric mixer for about 2 minutes until thickened, pale in colour and falling from the whisks in thick ribbons. Pour about 125ml of the cream mixture into the egg yolks and beat thoroughly.

Reheat the remaining cream until it just comes to the boil, then take it off the heat and stir it into the beaten egg and cream.

Return the mixture to the pan and cook very gently over a low flame, stirring all the time with a wooden spoon. Don't, whatever you do, let it boil. As soon as you see bubbles on the surface, it should be thick enough, so quickly take the pan off the heat so the mixture doesn't curdle. »

» Pour the custard into a heat-proof bowl, then sit it in a bigger bowl that is one-third full of iced water (that's why you need the ice cubes). Let it cool to room temperature, which will take about 20 minutes. Stir it again, remove the vanilla pod pieces, then place a piece of greaseproof paper or cling film directly on the surface of the custard to stop a skin forming. Put the bowl in the fridge for about 45 minutes until very cold, or overnight, if you prefer.

Slowly pour the cold custard into your ice cream maker and churn for roughly 20–30 minutes. While it's still a little soft, fold in the peanut butter and the toffee. Spoon the ice cream into a lidded plastic container, cover with cling film, then the lid, and freeze for a minimum of 3 hours.

Remove the ice cream from the freezer 15 minutes before serving.

Chocolate Chunk Cookies

There's nothing like having a big plate of cookies on the kitchen counter, ready and waiting for the kids' arrival, is there?

Makes 30

225g butter
225g granulated sugar
200g condensed milk
100g milk or white chocolate, chopped
100g dark chocolate, chopped
375g plain flour
2 teaspoons baking powder

Preheat the oven to 180°C/fan 160°C/gas mark 4. Line a couple of baking sheets with non-stick baking paper.

Cream the butter and sugar until light and fluffy. Add the condensed milk and chocolate and mix well. Add the flour and baking powder and combine.

Place about 30 spoonfuls of the mixture, spaced well apart, onto the prepared baking sheets. Press down on each heap with a fork. Bake for 20 minutes or until the biscuits are golden brown. Cool on a wire rack.

Crispy Crunchy Chocolate Popcorn Drops

Making these is messy fun and not for the faint hearted – it's guaranteed to give you a cleaning-up job, but the kids love making them, so it's worth the effort. You can leave out the nuts if anyone is allergic. The popcorn drops are just as good without.

Makes 24

350g milk chocolate (use any flavour you like, or try chocolate
   caramel chunks), chopped
120g toffee popcorn (or use 60g toffee popcorn and 60g plain popcorn)
240g chopped cashew nuts
Edible decorations of your choice

Line a 24-hole mini-muffin tin with paper muffin cases.

Melt the chocolate in a bowl set over a pan of simmering water, stirring every 30 seconds.

Place the popcorn and chopped nuts in a bowl and pour over the melted chocolate, stirring well until all the popcorn is evenly coated in chocolate.

Place spoonfuls of the mixture into the muffin cases and, before the chocolate has a chance to set, quickly add your decorations – sprinkles, mini marshmallows, chewy sweeties, small chocolate eggs … let your imagination run riot! Set aside until the chocolate has set.

Lashings of Ginger Beer

I know you can buy it, but it's such fun to make your own. We call it ginger bear – because it roars. The ginger must be very fresh and firm. No limp ginger, please.

Makes 2.5 litres

3 lemons, halved
75g fresh root ginger, grated
2 cloves
2 teaspoons cream of tartar
275g caster or granulated sugar
2.5 litres boiling water
1 x 7g sachet dried yeast

Put the halved lemons in a stainless steel bowl with the grated ginger, cloves, cream of tartar, sugar and boiling water. Stir thoroughly to dissolve the sugar, then leave to cool until the mixture is tepid. You should be able to dip your finger in comfortably.

Pour in the yeast, cover with cling film and set aside overnight. Next day, strain the liquid through muslin, pour it into clean bottles and stopper them.

Weekday Suppers

An evening meal during the working week has to be quick and easy to prepare – we all live life at a hundred miles an hour, and weekdays are all about having very little time and too much to do. We live in a world, thankfully, in which we have a gadget for everything, and kitchen gadgets make life much easier than in my nana's day. She would boil the bones of leftover chicken, turkey or beef to make stock for soups. Every part of an animal was used, so in her pantry she had plenty of choices and could make a quick meal out of anything. Now that we have every piece of equipment possible, we should be able to plan at least as well as my nana did for us. Preparing and cooking is a bit like gardening – when one thing is running low, make sure you have something else on its way. Stews, pies and burgers can be made beforehand and frozen, ready to be defrosted and heated through. And you can always make a double quantity and enjoy the same meal the next day. My dad often had a stew on the stove. He'd eke it out for a few days and make fresh dumplings for it every day. (We might find the idea of keeping a dish for days a bit distasteful now, but it never did us any harm.)

The recipes in this chapter require minimum fuss, yet will give you maximum enjoyment to nourish you after a long, hard day's work.

Scrumptious Sausage Supper

This is really just a posh version of everyone's favourite – sausage and mash. But the redcurrant sauce makes a traditional and well-loved supper dish that little bit extra special.

Serves 4

8 sausages (about 450g)
1 tablespoon sunflower oil
Sea salt and freshly ground black
   pepper

For the red wine sauce
300ml red wine
½ lamb stock cube
85g butter

For the redcurrant compote
15g butter
1 red onion, peeled and chopped

1 red pepper, deseeded and diced
2 tablespoons redcurrant jelly
3 tablespoons red wine
1 tablespoon red wine vinegar
2 tablespoons chopped coriander
   leaves

To serve
The Best Mash Ever (see page 158)
Stir-Fried Cabbage with Juniper
   Berries (see page 162)

Preheat the oven to 200°C/fan 180°C/gas mark 6.

Prick the sausages with a fork and place them in a roasting tin. Drizzle over the sunflower oil and season. Roast for at least 15 minutes, turning occasionally, until well browned and cooked through.

Meanwhile, prepare the red wine sauce. Place the wine and stock cube in a saucepan and bring to a simmer. Simmer until the wine has reduced by about a third.

As the wine sauce simmers, make the redcurrant compote. Melt the butter in a pan and cook the red onion and pepper over a medium heat for 5 minutes until softened. Stir in the redcurrant jelly, wine, vinegar and coriander and season with salt and pepper to taste. Simmer gently for 5 minutes then set aside.

Gradually whisk the butter into the reduced red wine to produce a smooth, glossy sauce. Season to taste.

Spoon the cabbage with juniper berries onto plates, place the sausages on top, then add the mashed potatoes and a dollop of redcurrant compote on the side. Pour over the red wine sauce and serve immediately.

Better Burgers

Burgers get a very bad press, but they needn't be heavy or fattening. Homemade, using good meat, well seasoned, freshly prepared and eaten quickly, they're delicious and good for you.

Serves 4

350g lean minced beef
225g turkey mince
2 tablespoons tomato purée
2 teaspoons Worcestershire sauce
1 teaspoon sea salt
1 teaspoon freshly ground black pepper
1½ teaspoons chopped rosemary leaves
1½ tablespoons olive oil
4 slices of mature Cheddar cheese
4 hamburger buns, split open
Handful of lettuce leaves (use a crisp variety, such as iceberg or Cos)
2 tomatoes, sliced and dressed with olive oil,
    balsamic vinegar, salt and pepper

To serve
Gherkins
Pickled onions

In a bowl, combine the beef, turkey, tomato purée, Worcestershire sauce, salt, pepper and rosemary. Divide the mixture into 4 equal portions and shape these into patties. Put the patties on a plate, cover with cling film and chill in the fridge for about 1 hour.

Heat the grill to a high setting. You can cook the burgers completely under the grill, or, alternatively on a griddle, then finish off under the grill. If you prefer to use a griddle for the first part of cooking, you'll need to preheat that, too. Brush each burger with olive oil and cook for about 6 minutes on each side. Place a slice of cheese on each burger and grill until the cheese has melted.

Place a burger on the lower half of each bun, add some crisp lettuce leaves and slices of tomato, then cover with the top half of the burger bun. Serve immediately, with gherkins and pickled onions on the side.

Perfect Potato, Cheese and Pickle Pie

This dish is like a jacket potato in a pie! It's very soothing, and I've found it is best eaten straight from the baking dish with a fork, in front of the fire, watching *Benidorm* on TV!

Serves 4

8 medium potatoes, peeled and diced
1 onion, peeled and diced
30g butter, plus extra for greasing
Milk
175g strong Cheddar cheese, grated
1 tablespoon Branston Pickle

Boil the potatoes and onion together in salted water until the potatoes are tender. While they are cooking, preheat the oven to 180°C/fan 160°C/gas mark 4. Grease a 23cm baking dish.

Once the potatoes are cooked through, drain them and the onion and mash them together with the butter and a dash of milk. Now slowly mix in 150g of the cheese and the pickle.

When everything is well combined, spoon the mixture into the prepared baking dish and sprinkle over the remaining cheese. Bake in the centre of the oven for about 20–25 minutes until the cheese has melted and the pie is piping hot and turning brown. Serve immediately.

Hearty Lamb Stew

This tasty stew is something that you can easily make ahead and store in the freezer, or take round to your hardworking daughter's house to pop in her freezer! It's lovely just as it is, but my dad, bless him, would have had dumplings with it.

Serves 6

Sea salt and freshly ground
    black pepper
25g plain flour
750g lamb neck fillet, cubed
1 tablespoon olive oil
50g butter
1 onion, peeled and diced
2 carrots, peeled and thickly sliced
Small glass of red wine
300ml stock (lamb, if you have it,
    but chicken is fine, too)

2 bay leaves
2 sprigs of rosemary

For the dumplings
125g plain flour
65g shredded suet
½ teaspoon baking powder
Pinch of salt
3–5 tablespoons cold water

Preheat the oven to 150°C/fan 130°C/gas mark 2. Season the flour and mix well. Toss the lamb in the seasoned flour.

Heat the olive oil in a heavy-based casserole, add the butter and then the lamb. Brown the meat all over. Remove the lamb from the pan and set aside.

Reduce the heat and cook the onion and carrots in the same pan for about 5 minutes until the onion is soft and translucent.

Add the wine, scraping the bottom of the pan well. Return the lamb to the pan and add the stock, bay leaves and rosemary. Bring the stew back to a simmer, then cover the casserole with a lid and put it in the oven for 40 minutes.

While it's cooking, make the dumplings. Mix the flour, suet, baking powder and salt in a bowl. Gradually add just enough of the cold water to form a sticky dough. Divide the dough into 12 pieces and form these into balls. Set aside.

Take the stew out of the oven, check the level of liquid, adding a little more stock if it seems too dry, then drop in the dumplings. Push them down a bit so that they're half submerged. Cover the pan with the lid and return it to the oven for another 20–30 minutes. Serve immediately.

Sunderland Hot Pot

This is a traditional Mackem recipe. (Mackems are people who, like my lovely dad, are Sunderland-born, and they should never be confused with Geordies from Newcastle.) It's a bit like a Lancashire hot pot, but is made with corned beef rather than lamb chops. You can cook it with or without dumplings, and you can add sausages to the dish to bulk it out if you like, too.

Serves 4

340g corned beef, sliced
½ onion, peeled and sliced
1 large baking potato,
    peeled and sliced
1 carrot, peeled and chopped
1 parsnip, peeled and chopped
1 celery stick, chopped
450ml gravy
Sea salt and freshly ground
    black pepper

1 tablespoon Worcestershire
    sauce (or to taste)

For the dumplings (optional)
125g plain flour
65g shredded suet
½ teaspoon baking powder
Pinch of salt
3–5 tablespoons cold water

Preheat the oven to 200°C/fan 180°C/gas mark 6.

Place a layer of corned beef in a medium-sized oven-proof dish. Add a layer of sliced onion, then a layer of potato, then carrots, parsnip, celery and any remaining onion. Top with a final layer of potatoes. Pour over the gravy. Season with salt, pepper and Worcestershire sauce, then pop the dish into the oven.

If you're having dumplings, make them now. Mix the flour, suet, baking powder and salt in a bowl. Gradually add just enough cold water to form a sticky dough. Divide the dough into 12 pieces and form these into balls. Set aside.

When the hot pot has been cooking for 35–40 minutes, remove the dish from the oven and add the dumplings, then cook for another 20–30 minutes until the dumplings are golden and crunchy. If you're not having dumplings, just continue to cook the hot pot until the potato topping is brown and crisp.

Traditional Corned Beef Hash

Simple, quick, cheap and very nutritious, we lived on this when I was at RADA. Corned beef went out of fashion for a while, although I'm not sure why. Perhaps it was because everyone thought red meat was too fatty. But we are over that now – we know that you should just eat it less often. This hash is so tasty and makes a cracking supper.

Serves 4

4 large potatoes, peeled and cubed
Butter, for greasing
1 tablespoon vegetable oil
1 onion, peeled and diced
1 red pepper, deseeded and chopped
340g can corned beef, chopped
Sea salt and freshly ground
   black pepper

150ml double cream
1–2 tablespoons creamed
   horseradish
Chopped flat-leaf parsley
   leaves, to garnish

Boil the potatoes in salted water until tender and drain well. Leave them to stand in the colander so that they dry out slightly.

Preheat the oven to 200°C/fan 180°C/gas mark 6. Lightly grease a medium-sized casserole dish with butter.

Heat the oil in a frying pan and add the onion and pepper. Cook over a medium heat for 5 minutes until the vegetables are soft.

Add the potatoes to the pan and cook over a medium heat, stirring frequently, for 10 minutes until the potatoes begin to turn brown. Stir in the corned beef and season to taste.

Whisk the cream and horseradish together, then fold the mixture into the hash.

Put the mixture into the prepared casserole dish and bake for 15–20 minutes until the hash is bubbling and beginning to brown. (If you prefer, you can top the hash with grated cheese and brown it under a hot grill.)

Take the hash out of the oven, scatter over the parsley and serve immediately.

Fabulous Fish Cakes

I love fish cakes – and they're surprisingly easy to make. You can start from scratch with raw fish, or do what I do and use leftover salmon. You can even buy ready-cooked salmon fillets now, too, which makes the recipe even easier. Serve up one or two per portion, depending on appetite, with a wedge of lemon, some chilli mayonnaise (a dollop of chilli sauce stirred into some good shop-bought mayonnaise), a green salad and some sweet potato fries.

Makes 4

350g potatoes, peeled and cut into chunks
450g salmon fillets, cooked
1 tablespoon chopped flat-leaf parsley leaves
½ teaspoon lemon zest
1 egg, beaten
85g fresh white breadcrumbs
Flour, for dusting
3–4 tablespoons vegetable oil, for shallow-frying

Boil the potatoes in salted water for 10 minutes or until they are tender but not breaking up. Drain them well, then return them to the pan and put it over the lowest possible heat for 1 minute to dry them out. Mash them with a fork so you have a dry, fluffy mash.

Flake the fish and mix it gently into the potato with the parsley and lemon zest. (If the mixture seems too dry, moisten it with a tiny bit of milk.) Set aside to cool.

Put the egg in a shallow bowl or large plate. Spread out the breadcrumbs on a baking sheet. Dust the work surface generously with flour.

Divide the fish mixture into 4 equal portions and shape these into patties on the floured work surface with floured hands. Dip each fish cake first into the egg, covering the sides as well, then into the crumbs, patting the crumbs all over the patty. Transfer to a plate, cover and chill for 30 minutes. You can leave them in the fridge overnight if you like.

Heat the oil in a large frying pan. When it's hot, fry the fish cakes over a medium heat until crisp and golden brown on both sides. Serve immediately.

Nana's House Pie

This is my version of a cottage pie and it's a child's delight – well, it is to my Oliver anyway. But grown-ups love it just as much, and it's simple to throw together, so it's a good one for after work or if the family suddenly pop over midweek. And the kids can help you make it, too.

Serves 4

1 tablespoon vegetable oil
2 onions, peeled and chopped
450g minced beef
1 tablespoon plain flour
450ml beef stock
1 tablespoon Worcestershire sauce
1 tablespoon tomato purée
Sea salt and freshly ground black pepper
900g potatoes, peeled and cut into chunks
25g butter
About 4 tablespoons milk

Heat the oven to 170°C/fan 150°C/gas mark 3½.

Heat the oil in a casserole dish and fry the onions over a low heat for 5 minutes. Increase the heat to medium, add the beef and cook until it just browns. Stir in the flour, stock, Worcestershire sauce and tomato purée. Bring the mixture to the boil and season, then cover with a lid, transfer to the oven and bake for 20 minutes.

Meanwhile, boil the potatoes in salted water until tender. Drain them and return them to the pan. Mash the potatoes with butter and a splash of milk, but don't overdo it – sloppy mash is unforgivable.

Remove the casserole from the oven, then increase the oven temperature to 220°C/fan 200°C/gas mark 7. Spoon the beef mixture into a medium pie dish and spread the mashed potato over the top. Bake for 25 minutes until the potato starts to brown. (If you like, add a sprinkling of grated cheese just before you're due to take it out of the oven and return the dish to the oven until the cheese is melted and bubbling.) Serve immediately.

Serious Steak and Kidney Pie

When I first left drama school I was lucky enough to be taken on by the most wonderful agent, Peter Eade. He used to take me to Rules in Covent Garden, one of London's oldest restaurants. This is my version of the classic pie that is always on their menu.

Serves 6

2 tablespoons vegetable oil
700g stewing steak, cubed
200g lamb's kidney, cubed
2 onions, peeled and diced
30g plain flour
850ml beef stock
Sea salt and freshly ground black pepper
Worcestershire sauce
500g puff pastry
Beaten egg, for glazing

Heat the vegetable oil in a large frying pan over a medium heat and brown the beef in it. Do it in batches so you don't overcrowd the pan. Set aside, then do the same with the kidneys. Add the onions to the kidneys in the pan and cook for another 3–4 minutes.

Return the beef to the pan, sprinkle with the flour and stir well to coat. Add the stock and season with salt, pepper and a dash of Worcestershire sauce. Stir well and bring to the boil. Reduce the heat to as low as it will go and simmer the stew, uncovered, for 1¼ hours. If it begins to look too dry, just add a little more stock.

Remove from the heat and taste to check the seasoning. Pour the mixture into a large pie dish and leave to cool.

Preheat the oven to 200°C/fan 180°C/gas mark 6.

Roll out the pastry and cut strips to line the rim of the pie dish. Brush the rim with water to wet it first, press on the pastry strips, then dampen the pastry strips, too. Cover the entire top of the pie with the remaining pastry. Trim off the excess pastry and crimp the edges with a fork or your thumb. Brush with beaten egg and bake for 30–40 minutes or until the pastry is well risen and a beautiful golden brown.

Comforting Chicken and Ham Pie

Everyone likes a good pie, piping hot with a golden pastry crust. This one never fails to please. It's especially good served with mashed potatoes and the lemony sugar snap peas on page 164, but it's just as nice with little new potatoes and frozen peas.

Serves 6

6 boneless, skinless chicken
   breasts, cubed
2 onions, peeled and chopped
3 carrots, peeled and sliced
2 celery sticks, finely chopped
2 teaspoons chopped thyme leaves
   (or 1 teaspoon dried thyme)
Sea salt and freshly ground
   black pepper
450ml chicken stock

50g butter
50g plain flour
300ml milk
Juice of 1 lemon
2 tablespoons chopped
   flat-leaf parsley leaves
4 thick slices of ham,
   cut into strips
500g puff pastry
Beaten egg, for glazing

Put the chicken into a large pan with the onions, carrots, celery, thyme and seasoning. Add the stock and bring to the boil. Reduce the heat and simmer very gently for 15 minutes. Strain the chicken and vegetables, reserving the stock. Set everything aside.

Rinse out the pan, then return it to the heat and melt the butter in it over a low heat. Stir in the flour to make a smooth paste. Add the stock a little at a time, stirring constantly to make a thick, smooth sauce. Now stir in the milk a little at a time. Take the pan off the heat, mix in the lemon juice and parsley and season to taste. Now add the reserved chicken and vegetables along with the ham and mix them in well. Pour the mixture into a large pie dish and leave to cool slightly.

Preheat the oven to 200°C/fan 180°C/gas mark 6.

Roll out the pastry and cut strips from the edges to line the rim of the pie dish. Brush the pastry rim with water, then cover the pie filling with the remaining pastry. Press it down well around the edges to seal the pie. Trim off any excess pastry, then crimp the edges with a fork or your thumb. Cut a hole in the middle to allow steam to escape. Brush the pastry with the beaten egg. Bake for 30 minutes until the pastry is a rich golden brown. Serve immediately.

Cidery Chicken Casserole

Everyone loves a good casserole and this one is quick, delicious and oh so comforting. As it's packed with veggies, all it needs on the side is some rice or some potatoes: boiled, mashed or baked – it's up to you!

Serves 6

1 tablespoon vegetable oil
6 chicken legs
1 leek, trimmed, washed and sliced
2 carrots, peeled and sliced
1 tablespoon plain flour
250ml dry cider
1 bay leaf
250ml chicken stock
Sea salt and freshly ground black pepper
1 tablespoon chopped flat-leaf parsley leaves
Boiled potatoes, mash or rice, to serve

Heat the vegetable oil in a wide casserole dish that will hold all the chicken legs in a single layer. Brown the chicken all over, remove from the pan and set aside.

Reduce the heat, add the leek and the carrots to the pan and turn to coat well in the remaining oil. Cook gently for about 5 minutes, then add the flour. Stir to mix well, then deglaze the pan with the cider.

Return the chicken legs to the pan and add the bay leaf and enough chicken stock to just cover them. Season with salt and pepper and bring to the boil. Reduce the heat and cover with a lid. Cook over a low heat for about 45 minutes.

Check to see that the chicken legs are cooked through and tender and check the seasoning. Take the pan off the heat, scatter over the parsley and serve the casserole with boiled potatoes, mash or rice.

Peppery Rocket Pasta

This is a far cry from your standard spag bol. It's a bit unusual and very tasty, but also a doddle to put together. It's perfect for a girls' night in, as it leaves you plenty of time to gossip.

Serves 2

250g fresh egg pasta
1 tablespoon butter
2 garlic cloves, peeled and crushed
Handful of rocket leaves

115g Parmesan or pecorino
  cheese, grated
Sea salt and freshly ground
  black pepper

Cook the pasta according to the packet instructions.

While it's boiling away, put the butter and garlic into a frying pan and cook over a medium-low heat until the garlic is just softened, but don't let it brown. Set the butter and garlic aside.

When the pasta is cooked, drain it well, return it to the pan and add the butter and garlic, rocket and cheese. Mix well and season to taste. Serve immediately.

Luscious Lasagne

For many people, lasagne is one of the first meals they learn to cook when they leave home, so start your kids off early and teach them how to do it now – it's fiddly but simple, and the results are truly luscious. Instead of making your own tomato and cheese sauces from scratch, you can always buy good-quality ready-made jars from the supermarket if time is limited.

Serves 6

10–12 sheets dried or fresh lasagne
100g grated Cheddar or other hard
  cheese
Parmesan cheese

750g lean minced beef
400g can chopped tomatoes
Sea salt and freshly ground
  black pepper

For the meat sauce
1 tablespoon olive oil, plus extra for
  greasing
1 red onion, peeled and chopped
4 rashers of smoked bacon, diced

For the béchamel sauce
1 tablespoon butter
1½ tablespoons flour
850ml milk

Preheat the oven to 180°C/fan 160°C/gas mark 4. Grease a 2 litre oven-proof dish with olive oil.

Heat the oil in a saucepan and cook the onion and bacon over a medium-low heat until the onion is translucent. Add the mince and cook until it browns. Mix in the chopped tomatoes and cook for 20–30 minutes until the sauce is thick. Season to taste.

In a separate pan, melt the butter and stir in the flour to make a roux. Now gradually add the milk, stirring constantly, until you have a thick white sauce.

To assemble the lasagne, place a layer of lasagne strips into the prepared dish, then add a layer of meat sauce, then a layer of béchamel sauce and a sprinkling of grated Cheddar cheese. Repeat until the dish is full, ending with a layer of lasagne sheets followed by one of white sauce. Scatter over any remaining cheese and grate over a generous amount of Parmesan.

Bake for 30 minutes until the lasagne is golden brown and crispy on top. Serve immediately.

Mega Mushroom Risotto

This is a dish I used to cook in my restaurant, one of our many veggie dishes. Sometimes I add chopped chilli or a splash of Tabasco for a little extra kick, but it's delicious as it is.

Serves 4

1.75 litres vegetable stock
15g dried ceps
85g butter
1 large onion, peeled and finely chopped
300g mixed wild mushrooms (such as ceps, chanterelles and
    oyster mushrooms), sliced
400g arborio rice
150ml dry white wine
60g Parmesan cheese, grated
Sea salt and freshly ground black pepper

Bring the stock to the boil in a large pan, then take the pan off the heat and soak the dried ceps in the stock for 20 minutes. Strain the stock and return it to the pan over a very low heat. Reserve the soaked mushrooms.

Heat half the butter in a saucepan and add the onion. Cook the onion over a low heat until it is soft and translucent. Add the fresh mushrooms, increase the heat and sauté until they are golden.

Add the rice to the pan and stir thoroughly. Now pour in the wine, increase the heat and simmer vigorously until the liquid has reduced by half, stirring constantly.

Put the soaked ceps into the pan, then gradually add the strained stock, a ladleful at a time, stirring constantly. After about 18 minutes, the rice will be firm but tender. Remove the pan from the stove and add the Parmesan and the remaining butter. Season to taste, cover and leave to rest for 4–5 minutes before serving.

Entertaining Family and Friends

I love dinner parties – dressing the table, decorating the house, planning the menu. I love having place cards so everyone knows where they are sitting. I like to mix it up so wives and husbands are separated – this doesn't always go down well, but I don't care. I always do a roast on a Sunday, and I think everything has its day, so friends coming over on a Monday would get a paella; on Wednesday, they'd be treated to sea bass; on Friday, my lucky guests would enjoy a big mustard steak and chips; and Saturday would be hot pot day. Talking of which, when I first joined the cast of *Corrie*, I had to stand at the bar of the Rovers for a scene that involved the character Betty Williams's famous hot pot. That lovely actress, Betty Driver, placed the hot pot in front of me, saying, 'Come on, kid, get stuck in.' I dutifully took a mouthful of hot pot. Betty and the cast and crew shouted, 'Nooooooo.' Too late – it was disgusting. 'They're just for show, love,' Betty said. 'They are sprayed with anti-shine, not to be eaten. I thought you knew.' I certainly did for the rest of that day!

The dishes in this chapter are the ones I love to share with my special guests, to make them feel welcomed and at home.

Posh Pepper and Goat's Cheese Lasagne

Everyone loves a traditional lasagne, like the one on page 129. This is more of a contemporary take on the Italian classic – and it's meat-free, so it's great if you are trying to cut down on your meat intake. It's also perfect for vegetarian guests.

Serves 6–8

Butter, for greasing
10–12 sheets dried or fresh lasagne
200g goat's cheese (about 1 log)
250g mozzarella (about 2 balls)
50g Parmesan cheese

1 tablespoon olive oil
Salt
400g tomato passata (about
   1 small carton)
240ml water

For the pepper sauce
1 onion, peeled and quartered
1 large green pepper,
   deseeded and quartered
1 large red pepper,
   deseeded and quartered

For the béchamel sauce
30g butter
3 tablespoons plain flour
850ml milk
Nutmeg

First make the pepper sauce. Blend the onion in a food processor until you have a thick pulp. Add the peppers and blitz them to a pulp with the onion.

Put the olive oil in a saucepan over a medium heat. Add the onion and pepper purée to the pan with a pinch of salt. Cook gently, stirring, for about 4 minutes. Pour in the passata and cook, still stirring, for another 4 minutes. Now add the water and simmer for 30 minutes, adding more water if the sauce becomes too dry.

While the pepper sauce is cooking, make a béchamel sauce. Melt the butter in a heavy-based saucepan. Stir in the flour to make a roux, then gradually add the milk a little at a time until you have a nice smooth sauce with no lumps. Add a good grating of nutmeg and a pinch of salt. Continue to cook on a low heat until the sauce has the consistency of custard. If it seems too thick, just add a little more milk to thin it to the right consistency.

Preheat the oven to 200°C/fan 180°C/gas mark 6. »

» Grease a 2 litre oven-proof dish, then cover the base with the pepper sauce. Add a layer of lasagne sheets. Pour in another layer of pepper sauce, then crumble over some goat's cheese and lay on slices of mozzarella. Cover with béchamel. Repeat until you have 4 layers, ensuring all the pasta sheets in each layer are covered with sauce. Finally, grate over the Parmesan.

Cover the dish with kitchen foil and place it on the middle shelf of the oven. Cook for 30 minutes. Remove the foil and put the dish back into the oven until the top of the lasagne is crispy and golden brown. Take the lasagne out of the oven and let it settle for a few minutes before serving.

Creamy Smoked Salmon Carbonara

If I ever get married again, the groom would be my best friend (and wonderful singer) Andrew Rodley – and this would be our wedding breakfast.

Serves 2

200g spaghetti
1 teaspoon butter
1 garlic clove, peeled and crushed
150ml double cream
2 eggs
30g Parmesan cheese, grated
120g smoked salmon, cut into strips (use trimmings, if you like)
½ small bunch of chives, chopped
Freshly ground black pepper, to serve

Cook the spaghetti according to packet instructions.

Meanwhile, melt the butter in a pan. Add the crushed garlic and allow the butter to sizzle for 1 minute then take the pan off the heat.

Lightly beat the cream, eggs, softened garlic and half of the Parmesan in a bowl. Stir in the salmon strips.

Drain the pasta, return it to the pan and add the salmon mixture with the chives, tossing well – the heat from the pasta will thicken the sauce slightly.

Serve with the remaining Parmesan and lots of freshly ground black pepper.

Crowd-Pleasing Kedgeree

This is such a versatile dish. Traditionally, it's eaten for breakfast, but these days, kedgeree is an anytime food. It seems to be a very old-fashioned English dish, but actually it's from India.

Serves 6

2 tablespoons vegetable oil
1 large onion, peeled and finely chopped
2 teaspoons Madras curry powder
Sea salt
300g long-grain rice
600ml water
300g smoked haddock fillet
6 peppercorns
2 bay leaves
300ml milk
4 eggs
Good handful of chopped flat-leaf parsley leaves
Large knob of butter

Heat the oil in a large lidded pan, add the onion and fry gently for 5 minutes until soft and translucent. Add the curry powder, season with salt and fry for about 3 minutes until the mixture begins to brown. Now add the rice and stir well. Pour in the water, stir again, then bring to the boil. Reduce the heat to the lowest possible setting, cover the pan with the lid and cook for 10 minutes. Take the pan off the heat and leave to stand, covered, for another 10–15 minutes, after which the rice will be perfectly cooked.

While the rice is cooking, put the haddock, peppercorns and bay leaves in a frying pan, cover with the milk and poach for 10 minutes or until the fish flakes easily. Remove the fish from the milk, peel away the skin and flake the flesh into large pieces, carefully removing any bones as you work. Discard the milk, skin and bay leaves.

Hardboil the eggs while the fish is cooking, too, then shell them and cut them into quarters.

When the rice is done, gently mix in the fish, then add the parsley and eggs and a generous knob of butter. Serve immediately.

Sea Bass with Mango and Chilli Salsa

This dish was a winner in the restaurant. Sea bass is one of the most gentle-flavoured fish, but the salsa really wakes it up – in the best possible way.

Serves 2

2 sea bass fillets
Olive oil, for frying

For the mango and chilli salsa
½ mango, peeled and chopped
2 spring onions, green and white parts chopped
1 red chilli, deseeded and chopped
Grated zest and juice of 1 lime
1 garlic clove, peeled and crushed
Sea salt

To serve
Lamb's lettuce
Coriander leaves
Vinaigrette of your choice

First make the salsa. Mix together the mango, spring onions, chilli, lime zest and juice and the crushed garlic. Season with salt to taste. Set aside.

Slash each of the sea bass fillets 3 times across the skin side. Dry the skin with kitchen paper.

Get a frying pan fairly hot, then add enough oil to cover the base of the pan. Let the oil become hot, then season with salt and reduce the heat to medium. Gently lay the fish fillets in the pan, skin-side down, and press down firmly with a fish slice. Cook, undisturbed, for 4 minutes, until the skin is crisp and golden. Don't fuss with the fish – let it form a crust. Turn the fish over, reduce the heat to low and cook for another 2 minutes.

Meanwhile, make a salad with the lamb's lettuce and coriander leaves and dress it with your favourite vinaigrette.

Once cooked, transfer each sea bass fillet to a plate and serve with the salsa and salad.

Crispy Parmesan Chicken on a Bed of Beef Tomatoes with Basil

As a kid, I could never work out which part of the cow beef tomatoes came from … duh! The tomato salad turns this relatively simple dish into something really quite sophisticated – and both children and adults seem to love it.

Serves 4

4 boneless, skinless chicken breasts
Plain flour, for dusting
85g breadcrumbs
55g Parmesan cheese, grated
1 teaspoon turmeric
1 red pepper, deseeded and
  very finely chopped
2 eggs, beaten
Olive oil and butter, for
  shallow-frying

For the tomato salad
½ tablespoon lemon-infused olive
  oil (or use plain olive oil)
2 teaspoons honey
2 garlic cloves, peeled and finely
  chopped
½ tablespoon balsamic vinegar
1 teaspoon brown sugar
Sea salt and freshly ground
  black pepper
4 beef tomatoes, sliced
Handful of basil leaves, torn

First, make the tomato salad. Mix the lemon-infused olive oil with the honey, garlic, balsamic vinegar, brown sugar and salt and pepper to taste. Put the tomato slices in a shallow bowl and pour the dressing over them. Throw the torn basil leaves into the bowl, then turn to gently mix the salad. Set aside.

Batter each chicken breast between 2 pieces of cling film until they are 1cm thick. Season with salt and pepper and dust with flour, tapping away any excess.

Mix the breadcrumbs, Parmesan, turmeric and chopped red pepper and spread out the mixture on a plate. Dip each piece of seasoned chicken in beaten egg, then into the breadcrumb mixture to coat.

Heat some olive oil with a knob of butter in a frying pan. Once it's sizzling, add the chicken and cook over a medium-low heat for 3–4 minutes on each side until crispy and golden.

Divide the tomato salad equally between 4 serving plates. Sit a piece of chicken on top of the tomatoes on each serving and sprinkle with a little sea salt. Serve immediately.

Really Garlicky Chicken Kiev

OK, this is garlic overkill, but feel free to adjust the quantity to your liking. Being me, I'd even serve it with extra garlic butter (using the recipe on page 168). As long as you're not snogging anyone that night, who cares? Garlic is so good for you.

Serves 4

4 boneless, skinless chicken breasts
Sea salt and freshly ground
   black pepper
3 garlic cloves, peeled and crushed
2 tablespoons fromage frais
1 tablespoon chopped flat-leaf
   parsley leaves

30g Parmesan cheese, grated
1 egg, beaten
30g golden breadcrumbs
Olive oil cooking spray

Preheat the oven to 190°C/fan 170°C/gas mark 5.

Slice lengthways along 1 edge of each chicken breast to open it out. Season inside the fold with salt and pepper.

Mix the garlic, fromage frais, parsley and 2 tablespoons of the grated Parmesan in a bowl. Spoon the mixture into the folds of the chicken breasts, then close up each breast and press down to seal. Skewer each breast with a cocktail stick to hold it shut, then place the breasts on a sheet of non-stick baking paper set on a baking tray.

Brush the base of each chicken breast with beaten egg and sprinkle lightly with breadcrumbs. Turn over and do the same to the top and sides, then sprinkle over the remaining Parmesan. Now give each breast a little blast of olive oil cooking spray.

Bake for 25–30 minutes until the chicken is golden brown and cooked through.

Roast Chicken and All the Trimmings

Roast chicken used to be a very rare treat, but nowadays we can enjoy it every Sunday if we want to. If possible try to buy free range and/or organic – at least you know the chicken has been treated well in its short life and the taste is so much better. Serve your roast chicken with pigs in blankets, your favourite vegetables, roast potatoes and bread sauce (see page 167).

Serves 6

1.5kg chicken
2 tablespoons olive oil
1 lemon
2 sprigs of tarragon
1 glass of dry white wine (or
    use sherry or cider)
500ml chicken stock
Sea salt

For the pigs in blankets
6 chipolata sausages
6 rashers of streaky bacon

For the roast potatoes
6 large potatoes,
    peeled and quartered
3 tablespoons vegetable
    oil or goose fat

Preheat the oven to 220°C/fan 200°C/gas mark 7.

To make the pigs in blankets, wrap 1 rasher of bacon round each sausage. Set aside.

Rub the chicken all over with the olive oil. Squeeze over the juice of the lemon and put the squeezed-out lemon halves into the cavity of the bird with the tarragon sprigs. Place the bird in a roasting tin and put it in the oven to roast.

After 15 minutes, add the pigs in blankets to the tin around the bird. Reduce the heat to 170°C/fan 150°C/gas mark 3½ and roast for a further 50 minutes.

As soon as the pigs in blankets go into the oven, start to prepare the roast potatoes. Parboil the potatoes for 5 minutes. Heat the oil or goose fat in a separate roasting tin, add the parboiled potatoes, turn them in the hot fat, then put the tin in the oven to cook the potatoes alongside the chicken.

When the chicken is cooked, remove the tin from the oven and increase the heat to 200°C/fan 180°C/gas mark 6 to crisp up the roasties. Transfer the chicken and the pigs in blankets to a serving plate and keep them in a warm place to rest for 15 minutes while you make the gravy.

Pour off any excess fat from the roasting tin you used to cook the chicken. »

» Place the roasting tin on the hob over a medium heat. Pour in the white wine and deglaze the pan thoroughly. Let the wine reduce a little, then add the stock. Bring to the boil then reduce the gravy until the flavour is nicely concentrated. Check the flavour and add salt to taste, then pour the gravy into a gravy boat.

When the potatoes are a lovely golden brown and crisp all over, take them out of their tin and serve everything up.

Super Spanish Paella

This is a regular on the lunch menu on the set of *Benidorm*. It's just as good back at home and a fabulously easy way to feed a crowd.

Serves 6

1 tablespoon olive oil
8 boneless chicken breasts and/or
   thigh pieces
1 onion, peeled and chopped
2 garlic cloves, peeled and
   finely chopped
100ml white wine
175g paella rice
500ml chicken stock

Pinch of saffron threads
1 tablespoon honey
200g ready-roasted peppers,
   drained and roughly chopped
100g fine green beans,
   trimmed and halved
2 tablespoons chopped flat-leaf
   parsley leaves, to garnish

Preheat the oven to 180°C/fan 160°C/gas mark 4.

Heat half the oil in a large, shallow casserole dish. Cut the chicken into bite-sized pieces, then brown it over a medium-low heat for a few minutes until golden on all sides. Remove the chicken pieces from the pan and set aside.

Add the remaining oil to the pan and soften the onion for 5 minutes. Stir in the garlic and cook for 1 minute. Pour in the wine and let it bubble for 2–3 minutes. Now add the rice, stock, saffron, honey, peppers and green beans and bring to the boil.

Put the chicken pieces in the casserole on top of everything else, cover tightly with the lid, then transfer the casserole to the oven and cook for 35–40 minutes until the rice is tender and the chicken is cooked through. Set aside to rest for 5 minutes, then garnish with the parsley and serve.

Minted Lamb Hot Pot

This isn't Betty Driver's famous hot pot from *Corrie*, but it is the hot pot we always had at home. My dad loved enormous bulbous pickled onions with this, the ones that shoot off the table when you try and stab them – always a source of amusement for the grandchildren.

Serves 6

6 lamb chops
30g butter, plus extra for greasing
Olive oil, for shallow-frying
3 onions, peeled and thinly sliced
2 carrots, peeled and thinly sliced
2 celery sticks, thinly sliced
Sea salt and freshly ground
   black pepper
6 potatoes, peeled and sliced
1 tablespoon Worcestershire sauce
425ml chicken stock
425ml beef stock

For the marinade
2 tablespoons olive oil
1–2 garlic cloves, peeled and crushed
Handful of mint leaves, chopped
1 tablespoon mint sauce

To serve
Pickled onions
Red Cabbage (see page 162)
French bread and butter

Mix the marinade ingredients together and season with salt and pepper. Put the chops in a dish and pour over the marinade. Rub it in well, ensuring the meat is thoroughly coated. Leave the dish in the fridge for several hours or overnight to allow the meat to marinate.

When you're ready to cook, preheat the oven to 180°C/fan 160°C/gas mark 4. Butter a large oven-proof dish that has a lid.

Heat the butter in a large frying pan set over a medium-low heat. Remove the lamb from the marinade and brown it in the frying pan for a few minutes, turning it all the time. Transfer the lamb to a plate and set aside.

Add a little olive oil to the pan and cook the onions gently until soft, then set aside. Now add the carrots to the pan, cook gently until soft and set aside. Do the same with the celery.

Now start layering the ingredients in the prepared oven-proof dish, seasoning with salt and pepper as you go. Put half the potatoes in the bottom of the dish in a single layer. Follow with a layer using half the onions, then the chops. »

» Add the remaining onions, then the carrots, then the celery. Cover with the remaining potatoes.

Mix the Worcestershire sauce with both stocks (add a dessertspoonful of mint sauce, if you like). Pour the mixture into the dish. Cover with the lid and bake for 1¾ hours.

Serve with pickled onions (little silverskin ones are good), steamed red cabbage and warm French bread with lashings of butter.

Marvellous Marrakesh Lamb

I once had a home in Spain. Morocco wasn't far away and my best friend John took me to Marrakesh; I've never forgotten the sounds, smells or atmosphere. I can't recreate the sounds or atmosphere, but I can try to give you the smells.

Serves 4

2 tablespoons olive oil
1 large onion, peeled and diced
1 teaspoon chilli powder
1 teaspoon ground cumin
1 teaspoon ground cinnamon
2 garlic cloves, peeled and crushed
450g lamb (shoulder or leg), cut into
   chunky cubes

120g dried apricots, chopped
1 tablespoon tomato purée
Grated zest and juice of 1 orange
850ml chicken stock
Sea salt and freshly ground
   black pepper
400g can chick peas, drained
Rice or couscous, to serve

Heat the oil in a heat-proof casserole dish and fry the onion gently until softened. Add the spices and continue to fry gently for 1 minute, then add the garlic and meat. Brown the meat on all sides.

Now add the apricots, tomato purée, orange zest and juice and the stock and season with salt and pepper. Bring the mixture to the boil, then cover with a lid, reduce the heat to the lowest possible setting and simmer for 1–1½ hours until the lamb is cooked.

Put the chick peas into the casserole and simmer for 5–10 minutes until they're heated through.

Serve immediately with rice or couscous.

Mighty Mustard Steak

I used to cook this at least once a week when I was married – usually a very large T-bone steak. If it seems simple, unfussy and non-fattening – well, apart from the chips – that's because that's exactly what it is. Enjoy.

Serves 4

4 thick sirloin steaks

For the marinade
2 tablespoons olive oil
2 tablespoons red wine vinegar
2 tablespoons Dijon mustard
2 teaspoons Worcestershire sauce

Pinch of thyme leaves
Sea salt and freshly ground black
  pepper

To serve
Perfect Chips (see page 160)
Watercress, to garnish

Whisk all the ingredients for the marinade together. Put the steaks in a shallow dish and pour over the marinade. Leave the steaks in the fridge to marinate for at least 30 minutes.

When you're ready to cook, heat a griddle pan until it's really, really hot (and be sure to have the extractor fan on full blast, too). Cook the steaks for 2 minutes per side for rare, 3 minutes per side for medium rare and 4 minutes per side for well done.

Leave the steaks to rest on hot plates for a few minutes then serve with chips and a bunch of watercress.

Beery Beef Pot Roast

When I was pregnant I was low in iron so the doctor suggested I drink Guinness, but the best and sweetest Guinness is in Ireland so I turned to Mackeson Stout instead. It's almost a meal in a glass, so I thought I'd start adding it to dishes I cooked at home. This is one of them and it's been a family favourite ever since. A good pot roast is such a comforting dish, especially if served with a pile of fluffy mashed potatoes and mushy minted peas.

Serves 6

1 tablespoon sunflower oil

1 tablespoon butter

900g beef brisket

2 onions, peeled and chopped

6 celery sticks, thinly sliced

450g carrots, peeled and cut into chunks

2 tablespoons plain flour

480ml beef stock

300ml stout (I use Mackeson Stout)

1 bay leaf

½ teaspoons dried thyme

1 teaspoon brown sugar

2 tablespoons Dijon mustard

1 tablespoon tomato purée

Sea salt and freshly ground black pepper

Boiled or mashed potatoes, to serve

Preheat the oven to 180°C/fan 160°C/gas mark 4.

Heat the oil and butter in a large casserole dish set over a medium-low heat and brown the meat on all sides. Remove the brisket from the pan and set aside.

Put the onions in the casserole and cook over a medium heat for 3–4 minutes, stirring constantly. Add the celery and carrots and cook for 3–4 minutes. Now add the flour, cook for 1 minute, then slowly add the stock and the stout, stirring constantly to blend the ingredients thoroughly.

Bring the mixture to the boil, still stirring, then reduce the heat to a simmer. Mix in the bay leaf, thyme, sugar, mustard and tomato purée and season to taste.

Put the brisket on top of the vegetables and cover the casserole with the lid. Transfer it to the oven and cook for 2½ hours or until the meat is fork-tender. Taste the gravy and adjust the seasoning as necessary. Add a pinch more sugar if needed.

Serve immediately, with boiled or mashed potatoes.

Coca-Cola Gammon with Caramelised Pineapple

Hutchinson stoppered bottles were used when the Coca-Cola Company first bottled Coke in the 1890s. Since my maiden name is Hutchinson, I somehow feel slightly proprietorial about Coke. And this recipe combines that sense of ownership with a childhood favourite. On Friday nights I'd be taken to the Berni Inn and gammon and pineapple was one of the things we always chose. Such a joy!

Serves 8

2kg gammon joint
1 litre Coca-Cola (about 2 small bottles)
2 tablespoons English mustard
3 tablespoons honey
½ ripe pineapple, peeled, cored and cut into 2.5cm-thick slices
Sugar, for sprinkling

Put the gammon in a large pot and pour over the Coca-Cola and enough water to cover the joint. Bring to the boil, then turn the heat to low and simmer for 2 hours. Remove the gammon from the liquid and leave to cool.

When it has cooled, strip the skin off the meat, then refrigerate it overnight.

Next day, when you are ready to cook, preheat the oven to 200°C/fan 180°C/gas mark 6.

Set the gammon in a roasting pan. Mix the mustard and honey together and spread the mixture over the meat. Cook for 1 hour. Take the joint out of the oven and let it rest for 20 minutes while you grill the pineapple.

Sprinkle the sugar over both sides of the pineapple rings. Heat a griddle pan until it is very hot and chargrill the pineapple slices for 3–4 minutes on 1 side until the sugar on the underside has caramelised. Turn the slices over and cook for a further 3–4 minutes until the slices are tender and golden.

Once the resting time is over, slice the gammon and serve it with the pineapple slices.

Super Sides

Whenever I go to a restaurant, side orders are really important to me. I think they should be interesting (look at bacony Brussels sprouts), comforting (try the best mash ever) and exciting (as is stir-fried cabbage with juniper berries). My mum only ever ate sides. She would say to the waiter, 'I'm a vegetarian and I only want side orders.' He'd point out that maybe a portion of chicken wings was not veggie, to which she'd say, 'Are you not listening? I'm vegetarian, I don't eat meat. Chicken isn't meat.' He'd go away thoroughly reprimanded and bring her the vegetarian chicken wings. So next time you're out at a restaurant, make sure you try the veggie meatballs!

Give your main dishes the support they deserve with these vital minor characters that bring magic to the entire show.

The Best Mash Ever

There's nothing like mashed potato piled high on your plate with a good lump of butter melting into it. I could happily eat it on its own, but it is, of course, perfect with stews, casseroles and roasts with lashings of gravy.

Serves 4

450g Maris Piper potatoes, peeled
Sea salt and freshly ground black pepper
4 tablespoons double cream
30g butter
1 tablespoon milk

Put the potatoes in a saucepan, cover with water and add 1 teaspoon salt. Bring to the boil, cover the pan with a lid and reduce the heat to a simmer. Cook the potatoes for 15–20 minutes until done.

Drain the potatoes and put them back into the pan for 1 minute or so to dry a little. Now add the cream and butter and mash, ensuring you get rid of any lumps. Add a splash of milk if the mixture seems too stiff, but don't make it wet. Dry, creamy mash is what you're after. Season with salt and freshly ground black pepper to taste, then serve immediately.

Crunchy Roast Potatoes

These are to die for. They are, quite simply, the best roast potatoes in the world. Yes, they're that good. Make sure you use a floury potato, such as King Edward or Maris Piper, for the best results.

Serves 6

1.75kg potatoes, peeled and quartered
2 tablespoons goose fat

Parboil the potatoes in salted water for about 7 minutes. Drain well and bash them about in the sieve or colander to fluff up the outsides.

While the potatoes are boiling, heat up your goose fat in a roasting tin in the oven – which is probably already nice and hot and cooking your Sunday joint or roast chicken. If you're just making the roasties, preheat it to 200°C/fan 180°C/gas mark 6.

When the fat is good and hot, tip the potatoes gently into the tin and turn them over to ensure they are well coated in the goose fat. Return the tin to the oven and cook for about 45 minutes or until the potatoes are crisp and golden. If they're not looking as crunchy and brown as you'd like them to be, leave them in for another 10–15 minutes. Remove from the fat with a slotted spoon and serve immediately.

Perfect Chips

Good chips depend on the potatoes you use – Maris Pipers are ideal.
I remember being with my dad, waiting in line in the warm, sizzling, steamy-windowed chip shop. The newspaper, the little white bag, then the freshly fried chips, lots of salt and vinegar and a little wooden fork. Heaven. When my nana made these at home when I was little, she always used beef dripping and her chips tasted amazing. These days, we do like to be a bit healthier, but it's worth falling off the wagon every now and then for these.

Serves 2

400g Maris Piper potatoes, peeled and cut into fat chips
Beef dripping (enough to half-fill your pan when melted)
Sea salt

Rinse the cut potatoes in water. Drain them then dry them well in a tea towel.
Heat the fat to 120°C. Add the chips (make sure you don't overcrowd the pan). Blanch them in the fat for about 5 minutes until cooked through but still pale – they mustn't colour. Remove the chips from the fat, drain them and pat them dry with kitchen paper.
At this stage, you can refrigerate the chips until you're almost ready to eat. When you are, heat the fat to 160°C and add the chips. Cook quickly until the chips are crisp and golden, then drain. Season with salt and serve straight away.

Stir-Fried Cabbage with Juniper Berries

I love cabbage, though I know many people, especially of my age, are still scarred by memories of school corridors reeking of overcooked cabbage. But when it's done properly, as here, it's delicious!

Serves 6

1 tablespoon olive oil
½ tablespoon butter
1 small Savoy cabbage, shredded
1 garlic clove, crushed

10 juniper berries, crushed
Sea salt and freshly ground
   black pepper

Heat the oil and butter in a large frying pan and stir-fry the cabbage and garlic for 4 minutes.

Stir in the juniper berries and salt and pepper to taste. Serve immediately.

Red Cabbage

This is a wonderfully tangy side dish – perfect with sausages and mash, or with either of the hot pots in this book.

Serves 6

1 small red cabbage, thinly sliced
1 tablespoon red wine vinegar
½ red onion, peeled and sliced
1 teaspoon redcurrant jelly

1 teaspoon brown sugar
1 tablespoon water
Pinch of salt

Mix all the ingredients together in a saucepan. Cover and bring to the boil. Cook over a medium-low heat for 10–15 minutes until the cabbage is cooked, but still has a bit of bite. Serve immediately.

Lemony Sugar Snap Peas

These go with pretty much everything – and I've yet to meet a child who didn't love them. They're perfect with the lemon fish fingers on page 94, but also with roasts and casseroles.

Serves 4

400g sugar snap peas
1 tablespoon olive oil
Sea salt and freshly ground black pepper
Grated zest of ½ lemon

Blanch the sugar snaps in salted boiling water for 20 seconds.

Mix the oil with some salt and pepper and the lemon zest. Drain the peas and drizzle over the seasoned oil. Serve immediately.

Quick Carrots

Like the lemony sugar snap peas above, these simple carrots are the perfect accompaniment to so many dishes. They're especially good with the roast chicken on page 144 – or with any roast, come to that.

Serves 4

450g baby carrots
30g butter
2 tablespoons honey
1 tablespoon lemon juice
Sea salt and freshly ground black pepper
Handful of chopped flat-leaf parsley leaves (or
   use basil, coriander or chives)

Cook the carrots for 5–6 minutes in salted boiling water.

Drain the carrots and return them to the pan with the butter, honey and lemon juice. Cook over a medium heat, stirring, for 5 minutes to glaze the carrots, then season and stir in the parsley. Serve immediately.

Bacony Brussels Sprouts

Sprouts, like cabbage, divide people. I love them, but they have to be properly cooked. If they're boiled to death and mushy, they're horrible! Lightly cooked, with a bit of bacon, on the other hand …

Serves 6

450g Brussels sprouts
225g bacon, chopped
6 shallots, peeled and sliced
60ml water
½ teaspoon thyme leaves
1 tablespoon balsamic vinegar
Sea salt and freshly ground black pepper

Wash the sprouts and make a single cut into the base of each one.

Brown the bacon in a large frying pan that has a lid, set over a medium heat, then add the shallots and sauté for a couple of minutes. Add the sprouts, water, thyme leaves, balsamic vinegar, and a pinch of salt and some black pepper. Cover with a lid and cook for 5 minutes until the sprouts are tender but not soggy. The water should have evaporated, but if not, increase the heat and cook until it has. Serve immediately.

Brilliant Bread Sauce

This is a great British classic, but like a lot of things it has lost its appeal over the years because people buy packet sauces and they're bland and boring. Homemade bread sauce is creamy and luscious and makes such a great accompaniment to roast turkey and chicken. Go on, bring it back to life.

Serves 6

400ml milk
1 onion, peeled and studded with 6 cloves
1 blade of mace
115g fresh white breadcrumbs
1 tablespoon double cream
25g butter
Sea salt and freshly ground black pepper
Pinch of cayenne pepper

Pour the milk into a saucepan and add the clove-studded onion and the blade of mace. Bring the mixture just up to the boil, then turn off the heat and leave to stand for about 30 minutes to allow the flavours to infuse the milk.

Discard the onion and the mace and bring the milk back up to the boil. Add the breadcrumbs and stir for about 5 minutes until they swell in the milk and the sauce thickens. If it's too thick, add a little more milk; if it's too thin, add a few more breadcrumbs.

Stir in the cream and butter and season with salt, pepper and cayenne. Serve immediately.

Garlic Bread

Everyone loves garlic bread, so it's good to have a special recipe for it up your sleeve. This garlic butter is also delicious simply poured over hot bread or jacket potatoes, or as an extra garnish for the chicken Kiev on page 143.

Serves 6

3–4 garlic cloves, peeled and crushed
115g butter, softened
Pinch of salt
Pinch of paprika
Squeeze of lemon juice
80ml olive oil
4–5 basil leaves, torn
1 large baguette or ciabatta

Preheat the oven to 200°C/fan 180°C/gas mark 6.

Add the garlic to the softened butter with the salt, paprika and lemon juice. Beat in the oil and stir in the torn basil leaves.

Halve the bread lengthways, then spread the garlic butter over both cut faces. Rejoin the bread into a loaf and loosely wrap it in kitchen foil. Pop it into the oven for 10 minutes. Open out the foil and continue to bake for 5 minutes until the crust is crispy.

Cut the bread into slices and serve immediately.

Raisin and Pine Nut Pilaf

A lovely accompaniment to so many things, but this side dish is especially good with the Marrakesh lamb on page 148.

Serves 4–6

2 tablespoons unsalted butter
1 small onion, peeled and finely chopped
½ teaspoon turmeric
¼ teaspoon ground coriander
200g long-grain rice
480ml chicken stock
4 tablespoons pine nuts, toasted
4 tablespoons raisins, soaked in boiling
   water for 1 minute and drained
Sea salt and freshly ground black pepper

Melt the butter in a heavy saucepan, add the onion with the turmeric and ground coriander and cook until the onion is soft.

Add the rice to the pan and stir to coat it well in the spiced butter and onion mixture. Add the stock, bring the liquid to the boil and simmer, covered, for 17 minutes or until the liquid is absorbed and the rice is tender.

Stir in the pine nuts and raisins, add salt and pepper to taste and serve immediately.

Proper
Puddings

Puddings are my downfall. When I ran my own restaurant in Richmond, Surrey, I always made my own banoffee pie, lemon meringue pie and hot white cheesecake. The problem is you can get fat making those kinds of puds – the cheesecake alone had about 2,000 calories.

When I left RADA I went to live with the legendary Joan Sims and she had a thing about spotted dick. It was often served at her dinner parties, of which there were many (mainly the Carry On crowd), and she always insisted that it was called spotty doggie – until she and Kenneth Williams got together. He would always tell her to stop being a silly person (I can't say what he actually said) and call it by its proper name – 'it's dick, Joanie, not doggie, for Gawd's sake.' It was delicious, whatever you called it!

Now a proper pudding is the right way to end a proper meal. The delicious offerings in this chapter won't disappoint you.

Crêpes with 43 Liqueur and Apples

As a kid I remember having flambéed crêpes with a warm orange sauce in restaurants with my parents. It was so exciting. The 43 Liqueur is from Spain and my mother always drank it with ice and Coca-Cola, so the smell reminds me of holidays. When I was filming *Benidorm* we all had a night out, and after much wine I was trying to explain it to Steve Pemberton, Jake Canuso and our writer, Derren Litten, but I kept calling it 45. The waiter had no idea what I was talking about, so after sampling every liqueur in the place we were not in a fit state to appreciate the 43 when at last the waiter found it. But it was a night!

Serves 6 (2 crêpes each)

1 large egg
300ml milk
125g plain flour
Pinch of salt
Pinch of caster sugar
Butter, for frying (about
   ½ teaspoon per crêpe)
Cream or ice cream, to serve

For the filling
25g butter
6 crisp eating apples (Cox or
   Braeburn are good), peeled,
   cored and quartered
2 tablespoons caster sugar
50ml Licor 43 Cuarenta Y Tres

First make the batter. Put the eggs, milk, flour, salt and sugar in a blender or food processor and whizz until smooth. If you want to make the batter by hand, put the dry ingredients in a bowl, make a well in the middle, break in the egg and add the milk. Whisk until smooth. Set aside while you make the filling.

Heat the butter in a frying pan and, when it's sizzling but not brown, add the apple. Reduce the heat and cook gently until the apple is soft. Add the sugar and coat the apple in it. Raise the heat a little and cook until the sugar has melted into the butter and the apple quarters begin to caramelise. Add the 43 Liqueur and bring to the boil to burn off the alcohol. Turn off the heat and keep warm while you make the crêpes.

Melt a tiny bit of butter in a clean frying pan. When it's just sizzling, pour in a thin layer of batter and swirl it around to cover the pan. Cook for a minute or 2. Check that the underside is nicely browned then flip it over with a spatula to cook the other side. Make another 11 crêpes with the remaining batter.

Fill each crêpe with a dollop of the apples and roll the edges over the filling. Serve 2 crêpes per person with cream or ice cream.

Very Berry Syllabub

Syllabub is a classic old English dessert that dates back to Tudor times, when it was served as a drink spiced with nutmeg. Today it's a rich, creamy dessert. I've always thought of it as a bit posh actually, perhaps because it was once served in royal circles.

Serves 6

250ml sweet white wine	150g blueberries
75g + 2 tablespoons caster sugar	150g raspberries
2 strips of lemon zest	150g strawberries
150g blackberries	600ml double cream

Combine the sweet white wine, 75g caster sugar and the lemon zest in a bowl. Stir to dissolve the sugar and leave to stand for 30 minutes to let the flavours infuse the wine.

Put the blackberries and blueberries in a saucepan and add 1 tablespoon caster sugar. Cook over a low heat until the fruit is tender and juicy. Push the mixture through a nylon sieve into a bowl to remove the seeds. Leave the purée to cool.

Blend the raspberries and strawberries in a blender with the remaining caster sugar until smooth. Again, push the mixture through a nylon sieve into a bowl to remove the seeds.

Remove the lemon zest from the wine mixture and discard.

Pour the cream into a bowl and whisk, adding the wine in a steady stream. Continue until the cream is soft and billowy.

Add two-thirds of each berry mixture to the cream and fold it in. Spoon the mixture into glasses and top with a drizzle of the remaining berry purées. Chill for a couple of hours, or overnight, until ready to serve.

Rhubarb Fool with Ginger Biscuits

This is a classic dish and very easy to make. You can use good ready-made biscuits, but making your own is even better. If you like, you can decorate them with icing – the kids always love doing this!

Serves 4

250g rhubarb, cut into chunks
125g caster sugar
300ml double cream

For the biscuits
350g plain flour
½ teaspoon ground ginger

1 teaspoon bicarbonate of soda
100g butter, plus extra for greasing
175g soft light brown sugar
3 tablespoons golden syrup
1 egg, beaten

Put the rhubarb and the caster sugar in a saucepan with just enough water to cover the rhubarb. Cover the pan with a lid and cook gently for 10 minutes or until the fruit is soft. Taste for sweetness and add more sugar if necessary. Drain the liquid from the fruit and leave to cool.

Whip the cream until it forms soft peaks. Gently fold the fruit into the whipped cream, but not so thoroughly that you can't see the pieces of fruit. Spoon the mixture into serving dishes and refrigerate until needed.

Now make the biscuits. Preheat the oven to 190°C/fan 170°C/gas mark 5. Grease a couple of large baking sheets.

Put the flour, ginger and bicarbonate of soda in a bowl and rub in the butter. Mix in the sugar, then the syrup and beaten egg, to make a firm dough.

Roll out the dough to a thickness of 5mm. Use a biscuit cutter to cut out any shapes you like from the dough – gingerbread men, stars, crescent moons, etc. Place the biscuits on the prepared baking sheets, ensuring they are well spaced out, and bake for 10–15 minutes until golden brown.

Leave the biscuits on the baking sheets to cool down for a few minutes to let them firm up, then place them on a wire rack to cool completely.

Serve the fool with the ginger biscuits alongside.

Tempting Tiramisu

This pudding varies such a lot but my lovely friend Michael Rivelli makes the best ever: soft, moist and with a kick – Italy brought to your table. But then, he *is* Italian.

Serves 6

180ml espresso or strong black
  coffee
500g mascarpone
6 eggs, separated

5 tablespoons caster sugar
200g sponge finger biscuits
2–3 bars of Cadbury's Flake

Pour the coffee into a flat dish. Set aside.

Beat the mascarpone in a bowl until smooth. Add the egg yolks and sugar and beat them into the mascarpone.

Whisk the egg whites until they are nice and firm, then fold them into the mascarpone mixture. Don't overdo it with the folding in – the mixture should be light and fluffy.

Soak the sponge finger biscuits 2 at a time in the coffee. Ensure they're covered, but don't let them soak for long enough to become soggy or they'll fall apart.

Spread a layer of the mascarpone mixture over the bottom of a rectangular dish that's roughly 23 x 30cm. Cover with a layer of coffee-soaked biscuits, then another layer of mascarpone. Repeat until you have reached the top of the dish, ending with a layer of mascarpone.

Crumble the Flakes over the top of the finished dish. Cover in cling film and refrigerate for at least 1 hour before serving.

Sublimely Sticky Toffee Pudding

People who came to my restaurant for Sunday lunch loved this dish, which is a proper tummy filler. You could see they had had a good Saturday night out, and they needed my pudding to warm their cockles and give them a little boost. They looked revived afterwards, ready for a sleepy afternoon in front of the telly, satisfied and very happy.

Serves 6

Butter, for greasing
190g plain flour
Pinch of sea salt
1½ teaspoons baking powder
120g soft light brown sugar
120ml milk
2 eggs
2 teaspoons vanilla extract
6 tablespoons melted butter

For the toffee sauce
120g butter
200g soft light brown sugar
450ml double cream

For the banana cream
1 ripe banana, sliced
60ml peach juice
30g sifted icing sugar
200ml double cream, whipped
¼ teaspoon vanilla extract

Make the banana cream first. Put the banana, peach juice and sugar in a pan. Cook over a medium heat for about 3 minutes until the banana is soft.

Transfer the mixture to a food processor and purée until smooth. Transfer to a bowl, cover and refrigerate for about 1 hour until cold.

Beat the cream until soft peaks form. Fold the cold banana purée into the cream. Stir in the vanilla. Cover and refrigerate until shortly before serving.

Preheat the oven to 170°C/fan 150°C/gas mark 3½. Grease a 1.5 litre baking dish.

Sift together the flour, salt, baking powder and sugar in a bowl. In a separate bowl, combine the milk, eggs, vanilla and melted butter and whisk until frothy. Add the mixture to the flour and mix until smooth. Pour the mixture into the prepared baking dish and bake for 20–30 minutes until the cake is firm on top.

Meanwhile, make the toffee sauce. Put the butter, sugar and cream in a pan and cook over a medium-high heat until the sauce is smooth and dark brown. Leave to stand for at least 10 minutes. When the cake has finished cooking, pour the toffee sauce over it and return it to the oven for 5 minutes until bubbling.

Serve the pudding in slices with a generous spoonful of the banana cream.

Nana's Sunday Specials

Every Sunday my nana brought these coconut and jam tarts over for tea and I always tried to eat them all. I would have killed my brother for his share – and I very nearly did.

Makes approximately 18

For the pastry
175g plain flour, plus extra for
  dusting
Pinch of salt
75g butter, plus extra for greasing
25g caster sugar
1 egg yolk

For the filling
6 teaspoons strawberry jam
150g butter
150g caster sugar
3 eggs, beaten
150g desiccated coconut
1 tablespoon plain flour

Preheat the oven to 180°C/fan 160°C/gas mark 4. Grease the holes of two 12-hole bun tins.

First make the pastry. Put the flour and salt into a large bowl. Rub in the butter until the mixture looks like breadcrumbs. Stir in the sugar, then make a well in the centre. Mix in the egg yolk and some ice-cold water, a little trickle at a time, until you have a firm dough.

Turn out the dough onto a floured board and knead lightly for 1 minute. Then roll out the dough until it is around 2mm thick and use a pastry cutter to cut out rounds. Put 1 circle into each of the holes of the bun tins. Spoon a generous ½ teaspoon jam into the centre of each circle. Set aside while you make the rest of the filling.

Cream the butter and sugar together until pale and fluffy. Gradually mix in the beaten egg (if the mixture looks as if it might curdle, add 1 teaspoon flour). Mix the coconut and the flour together and fold this into the mixture. If the filling is too stiff, add a drop of water to give it a soft consistency.

Using a teaspoon, spoon the mixture onto each of the dough circles in the tins over the jam. Do not overfill, as the filling needs room to rise.

Bake for 15–20 minutes until the pastry is golden and the filling is firm to the touch.

Take the tarts out of the oven, leave them to cool in the tins for 5 minutes, then transfer them to a cooling rack and leave to cool completely.

Egg Nog Custard Pie with Cherry Brandy Sauce

This was always brought out on special occasions at my nana's house. And there was a bottle of egg nog, a bottle of cherry brandy and, of course, bottles of the obligatory sherry (Harvey's Bristol Cream for the men; Croft Original for the ladies). This comical parade of bottles mocked my grandad, who would be in big trouble if he was ever caught with a beer at such an occasion. It's also comical that the contents of the bottles were not considered properly alcoholic, probably because they were only brought out on high days and holidays. And as far as my nana was concerned, this egg nog pie was also entirely booze-free. Just as my mum was convinced that chicken wasn't meat …

Serves 6

1 sheet of ready-rolled shortcrust pastry (or make your
   own, like my nana did – you'll need 250g)
Plain flour, for dusting
4 eggs
250g caster sugar
120ml egg nog, or more, to taste (I usually use Advocaat,
   but use whichever brand you prefer)
410g can evaporated milk
Pinch of nutmeg
Pinch of ground cinnamon

For the cherry brandy sauce
450g cherries (you could also use a 425g can of cherries)
1 cinnamon stick
1 tablespoon cornflour
1 tablespoon cold water
200g caster or granulated sugar
4 tablespoons cherry brandy

Preheat the oven to 180°C/fan 160°C/gas mark 4.

Dust the ready-rolled pastry sheet with flour and press it into a 23cm pie dish. Prick it all over with a fork. Cover the pastry dough with non-stick baking paper or kitchen foil, then pour in dried beans or ceramic baking beans. Bake for 20 minutes, then remove from the oven.

Beat the eggs and the sugar with a hand-held electric mixer set to a medium speed until light and fluffy. Add the egg nog and evaporated milk and mix well. Pour the mixture into the pastry shell. Sprinkle the nutmeg and cinnamon over the top. Bake for 1 hour. Test with a cocktail stick. If it comes out clean, it's done. Remove from the oven and leave to cool.

Meanwhile, make the sauce. Wash and stone the cherries. Put them into a saucepan with the cinnamon stick and add just enough water to cover them. Bring to the boil, then reduce the heat and simmer for 1 hour, after which you should discard the cinnamon stick.

Drain the cherries, reserving the liquid, and put them into a bowl. Return the liquid to the pan and bring to the boil. Mix the cornflour with the cold water and add the mixture to the cherry juice with the sugar. Stir to dissolve, then cook for 5 minutes, stirring constantly. Remove from the heat, stir in the brandy and pour over the cherries.

Serve generous slices of pie with the cherry brandy sauce.

Sherrie's Sherry Trifle

I can never resist a trifle – the layers, the colours, the occasion, and you can add so many things in endless combinations. There's nothing like a trifle to make you feel festive. You can have them all year round, but I save the all-singing, all-dancing one for Christmas. One Christmas Day I was walking in, holding the trifle high to present it to my family, and I tripped on the carpet and literally threw the trifle over everyone. We ended up spooning it off one another.

Serves 6

5 trifle sponges
55ml sherry
3 tablespoons raspberry jam
2 bananas, thinly sliced
250ml double cream
30g toasted almond flakes

For the custard
3 egg yolks
25g caster sugar
1 teaspoon cornflour
250ml milk
1 vanilla pod

Tear the trifle sponges into large pieces and put them into the bottom of a large, pretty glass bowl. Sprinkle with the sherry. Leave to soak while you make the custard.

Beat the egg yolks, sugar and cornflour together in a bowl. Put the milk and vanilla pod into a saucepan and bring it just to the boil. Take the pan off the heat and pour the milk over the egg, sugar and cornflour mixture. Return the mixture to the pan and cook the custard over a very low heat, stirring constantly, until it thickens and coats the back of the spoon. Take the pan off the heat, discard the vanilla pod and set aside.

Spread the jam over the soaked trifle sponges. Scatter the banana slices over the top of the jam. Now pour over the custard and leave to set.

Whip the cream until soft peaks form, then spoon it over the custard. Scatter the almonds over the cream. (If you prefer, use silver balls, hundreds and thousands or crystallised rose petals.) Chill the trifle until ready to serve.

Rocking Raspberry and Redcurrant Pie

A good fruit pie takes me right back to my nana's house. So many people grew fruit in their back gardens then and the kids would be sent out to pick it just before it was needed for the pie. Wonderful!

Serves 6

130g wholewheat flour
130g plain flour
1 teaspoon salt
115g very cold butter, cubed, plus
  extra for greasing
4–5 tablespoons ice-cold water
Cream or ice cream, to serve

For the filling
500g raspberries
125g redcurrants or
  blackcurrants, destalked
135g caster sugar
4 tablespoons plain flour
1 teaspoon lemon or lime juice

Mix the flours and the salt in a large mixing bowl. Using a round-ended knife or a pastry cutter, mix in the butter. Gradually add the water – don't put it all in at once or the dough will become too wet. You want just enough to ensure that the pastry comes together into a ball.

Wrap the pastry in cling film and rest it in the fridge while you preheat the oven to 220°C/fan 200°C/gas mark 7. Grease a 23cm pie dish or tart tin.

Roll out the dough and line the prepared tin with it. Reserve the trimmings to make the lattice top.

Mix the fruit with the sugar, flour and lemon or lime juice in a bowl. Mix well until all the sugar and flour has been absorbed into the fruit. Pile the fruit into the pastry shell.

Roll out the remaining dough and cut it into strips. Weave these into a lattice top for the pie, pressing down the strips at the pie edges to hold them in place.

Bake for 30 minutes, then reduce the heat to 180°C/fan 160°C/gas mark 4 and bake for another 30 minutes until the crust is golden brown and the filling cooked and set.

Serve hot or cold, with cream or ice cream.

Jolly Jam Roly-Poly

You can make this with the kids – you may not get an even roly, but who cares? They love it. At school we called this dish Dead Man's Leg. Well, you know what kids are like. It's not exactly an appetising name, but it's yummy, whatever you call it.

Serves 6

Butter, for greasing
150g self-raising flour, sifted, plus
   extra for dusting
75g shredded suet

Pinch of salt
100ml cold water
5 tablespoons raspberry jam
Custard, to serve (see page 184)

Preheat the oven to 200°C/fan 180°C/gas mark 6. Lightly butter a large sheet of non-stick baking paper.

Mix the flour, suet and salt together in a large bowl. Add just enough of the cold water to make a soft but not sticky dough. Turn out the dough onto a floured work surface and knead for a few minutes. Now roll out the dough into a square that's roughly 20 x 20cm and 1cm thick.

Spread a thick layer of jam over the dough, leaving a border of at least 1cm. Dampen the edge with a little water. Roll up loosely, pinching the ends together as you go to stop the jam from escaping. Place the roly-poly on the prepared baking paper with the sealed edge facing down. Fold over the ends of the paper and pleat it shut. Twist the ends like a sweetie wrapper and put the parcel on a baking tray.

Fill a roasting tin with boiling water and put it on the bottom shelf of the oven. Put the roly-poly on the top shelf and bake for 35–40 minutes.

When it's cooked, remove it from the oven, unwrap it and serve it in thick slices with custard.

Cider Chocolate Pears

This gorgeous twist on Pears Belle Hélène, the French bistro classic, is a brilliant pudding for a dinner party, or for a family lunch. Simple and delicious.

Serves 6

6 pears
3 tablespoons brown sugar
300ml sweet cider
Grated zest of 1 lemon
1 large strawberry, sliced, to decorate

For the chocolate sauce
150ml double cream
200g dark chocolate, finely chopped

Preheat the oven to 150°C/fan 130°C/gas mark 2.

Peel the pears, but leave the stems intact. Arrange them upright in a casserole dish that will hold them all snugly. Sprinkle over the brown sugar and pour over the cider. Scatter over the lemon zest. Bake for 1½ hours, covered with kitchen foil, then remove the dish from the oven and leave the pears to cool.

Gently transfer the pears to a serving dish and reserve the syrup.

Make the chocolate sauce. Pour the double cream into a saucepan and heat gently to scalding point. Take the pan off the heat and add the chocolate. Stir vigorously to make a smooth sauce.

Meanwhile, gently heat the syrup. When it is hot, pour it round the pears in the serving dish, then pour the hot chocolate sauce over the top of the pears. If you like, decorate the dish with slices of strawberry for colour. Serve immediately.

Angel's Mousse with Devil's Sauce

This white chocolate mousse with rich dark chocolate sauce makes a truly heavenly pudding – with a little gingery kick to warm you up on cold winter nights.

Serves 6

300g good-quality white
   chocolate, chopped
3 egg yolks
100g caster sugar
150ml milk
1½ leaves of gelatine
500ml double cream
Chocolate-covered crystallised
   ginger, chopped, to serve

For the sauce
150g dark chocolate,
   broken into small pieces
50ml whipping cream
2 tablespoons golden syrup
Knob of butter
Pinch of salt

First make the mousse. Melt the white chocolate in a heat-proof bowl set over a pan of simmering water, ensuring the base of the bowl isn't sitting in the water.

Meanwhile, whip the egg yolks and sugar in a bowl until the mixture is light and thick. Bring the milk to the boil, then take the pan off the heat and stir the milk into the egg yolk and sugar mixture and add the melted white chocolate. Put the mixture into the milk pan and stir over a very low heat until the custard starts to thicken. As soon as it begins to thicken, strain the mixture into a bowl.

Soak the gelatine leaves in a little water until softened. Squeeze out the water and add the gelatine to the warm custard. Mix well and leave to cool.

Whip the cream until it is soft and thick, then fold it into the chocolate custard. Spoon the mousse into 6 individual moulds and chill until set.

Make the chocolate sauce when it's nearly time to serve. Put the dark chocolate and whipping cream into a pan set over a very low heat. Stir until melted together. Add the syrup, butter and salt, beating well to make a smooth, glossy sauce. Keep the sauce warm until you're ready to serve.

Run a knife around the edge of each mousse in its mould and turn it out onto a serving plate. Drizzle chocolate sauce over each serving and decorate with chopped chocolate ginger, then serve immediately.

Index

Acknowledgements

This book is for my nana, who I'll never forget, and for all you other nanas out there.

It is also dedicated to my amazing daughter, Keeley, the love of my life and truly my gift from the stars above, and to my much-loved grandchildren, Oliver and Molly, two perfect little people who make my heart beat with joy every day. One day both Keeley and Molly will be nanas themselves, and what a lovely role that is.

All you nanas out there, never forget how important you are: you shape lives, teach life lessons and impart wisdom, and if you can do that whilst cooking together with your grandkids or dropping off a meal for a stressed-out mum – well, there's nothing more fulfilling ... apart from maybe one of my pies!

Outside the kitchen, I'd like to thank my lovely publishers, Pan Macmillan, especially Ingrid and George for being so brilliant, and also my agent Neil Howarth at Urban Associates for always believing in me and never doubting I could produce such a beautiful book – even when I disappeared to film *Benidorm* for five months just before I was due to finish it!

And a special thank you also goes out to all the foodie friends of mine all over the country who helped me to bring to you *Nana's Kitchen* by tasting and testing my recipes too!